T0372327

Cambridge Elements ☰

Elements in Epistemology
edited by
Stephen Hetherington
University of New South Wales, Sydney

KNOWING WHAT IT IS LIKE

Yuri Cath
La Trobe University

CAMBRIDGE
UNIVERSITY PRESS

Shaftesbury Road, Cambridge CB2 8EA, United Kingdom

One Liberty Plaza, 20th Floor, New York, NY 10006, USA

477 Williamstown Road, Port Melbourne, VIC 3207, Australia

314–321, 3rd Floor, Plot 3, Splendor Forum, Jasola District Centre,
New Delhi – 110025, India

103 Penang Road, #05–06/07, Visioncrest Commercial, Singapore 238467

Cambridge University Press is part of Cambridge University Press & Assessment,
a department of the University of Cambridge.

We share the University's mission to contribute to society through the pursuit of
education, learning and research at the highest international levels of excellence.

www.cambridge.org
Information on this title: www.cambridge.org/9781009500500

DOI: 10.1017/9781009323758

© Yuri Cath 2024

This publication is in copyright. Subject to statutory exception and to the provisions
of relevant collective licensing agreements, no reproduction of any part may take
place without the written permission of Cambridge University Press & Assessment.

When citing this work, please include a reference to the DOI 10.1017/9781009323758

First published 2024

A catalogue record for this publication is available from the British Library

ISBN 978-1-009-50050-0 Hardback
ISBN 978-1-009-32373-4 Paperback
ISSN 2398-0567 (online)
ISSN 2514-3832 (print)

Cambridge University Press & Assessment has no responsibility for the persistence
or accuracy of URLs for external or third-party internet websites referred to in this
publication and does not guarantee that any content on such websites is, or will
remain, accurate or appropriate.

Knowing What It Is Like

Elements in Epistemology

DOI: 10.1017/9781009323758
First published online: December 2024

Yuri Cath
La Trobe University
Author for correspondence: Yuri Cath, y.cath@latrobe.edu.au

Abstract: What kind of knowledge does one have when one knows what it is like to, say, fall in love, eat vegemite™, be a parent, or ride a bike? This Element addresses this question by exploring the tension between two plausible theses about this form of knowledge: (i) that to possess it one must have had the corresponding experience, and (ii) that to possess it one must know an answer to the 'what it is like' question. The Element shows how the tension between these two theses helps to explain existing debates about this form of knowledge, as well as puzzling conflicts in our attitudes towards the possibility of sharing this knowledge through testimony, or other sources like literature, theories, and simulations. The author also offers a view of 'what it is like' knowledge which can resolve both the tension between (i) and (ii), and these puzzles around testimony.

This Element also has a video abstract: www.cambridge.org/EEPI-Cath

Keywords: 'what it is like' knowledge, conscious experience, testimony, imagination and simulation, theories of knowledge

© Yuri Cath 2024

ISBNs: 9781009500500 (HB), 9781009323734 (PB), 9781009323758 (OC)
ISSNs: 2398-0567 (online), 2514-3832 (print)

Contents

1 Introduction

For any type of experience – be it momentous, amusing, traumatic, entertaining, or just trivial – we can identify a corresponding form of knowledge about *what it is like* to have that experience. So, not only can we experience grieving, falling in love, eating durian, seeing something red, being a parent, smelling a skunk, sitting in an anechoic chamber, or riding a bike, but we can also know what it is like to grieve, fall in love, eat durian, see something red, be a parent, smell a skunk, sit in an anechoic chamber, or ride a bike. What is involved in possessing this 'what it is like' knowledge? How is such knowledge gained, retained, and shared? And how does it relate to other forms of knowledge?

These are the central questions this Element will address, and these are all epistemological questions, as they concern the nature and character of a certain form of knowledge. However, when such questions are discussed, it is normally within the context of debates in the philosophy of mind, not epistemology. This is because claims about 'what it is like'-knowledge ('WIL-knowledge' or 'knowing-WIL' for short) have played a central role in debates about the nature of phenomenal consciousness, especially in connection to Jackson's (1982) knowledge argument against physicalist theories of consciousness. And outside of the philosophy of mind claims about the nature of WIL-knowledge have also played notable roles in other areas including transformative experiences (Paul 2014, 2015a), the philosophy of religion (Zagzebski 2008), and moral philosophy (Grace-Chappell 2017).

Many important ideas and theories about WIL-knowledge have been advanced in these areas, especially in relation to the knowledge argument, and some of these ideas and theories will be significant characters in the discussion to come. But my approach to thinking about WIL-knowledge will be somewhat different than the usual approach taken in discussing this topic. This is because I want to think about WIL-knowledge, first, as a topic of intrinsic interest within epistemology, rather than approaching it as primarily a topic of applied interest in relation to other areas of philosophy. A lot can be learned about WIL-knowledge by thinking about how it relates to these applied issues, but, equally, I think a lot can be learned by selectively bracketing those issues and considering WIL-knowledge more on its terms, and in relation to connected issues not only in the philosophy of mind but also in epistemology.

To clarify this difference in approach, recall Jackson's famous thought-experiment of the super-scientist Mary who knows all possible physical truths, including all the physicals truths about what goes on in a human brain when have visual experiences. However, despite having excellent vision herself, Mary has never had any experiences of seeing something red, as she has been kept her whole life in a room where she can only have black-and-white visual experiences. One day

Mary is released from her room and she sees something red for the first time and, thereby, comes to know what it is like to see something red. Jackson's knowledge argument then goes (roughly) like this: pre-release Mary knew all the physical truths, but there was at least one truth (namely, what it is like to see something red) that pre-release Mary was ignorant of before leaving her room, therefore, physicalism (understood as the view that all truths are physical truths) is false.

Probably the most noticeable way in which my approach will differ from most existing discussions of WIL-knowledge is that my ultimate aim is *not* to offer a response to Jackson's knowledge argument, or an analysis of what happens to Mary when she leaves her black-and-white room. The views about WIL-knowledge that I will go on to discuss and advance will have implications for how one evaluates that argument, and I will sometimes comment on those implications when relevant, but these views are not developed with such implications in mind.

From the perspective of a philosopher of mind interested in debates about the nature of phenomenal consciousness, such possible implications would understandably be their main concern, given the huge role that the Mary thought experiment has played in such debates. But from the perspective of an epistemologist, who wants to understand the nature of a given form of knowledge, it would be odd, and perhaps even methodologically suspect, to let these possible implications play a major role in guiding one's theorising about that form of knowledge. And while our intuition that Mary would gain new WIL-knowledge when she leaves her room is one interesting 'data point' that one might want one's theory of WIL-knowledge to accommodate, it is not more than that and there are other more humdrum and less contentious thought-experiments which provide similar lessons for our theories about WIL-knowledge. Relatedly, when Jackson's Mary is mentioned in the discussion to come, in most cases she could be replaced with Paul's (2014: 9) less tendentious character of 'ordinary Mary' who is not omniscient with respect to all the physical facts, but just has more normal levels of knowledge about the human brain and colour perception, and so on. So, while Mary will be a notable character in the discussion to come – this is unavoidable given how central she is to many existing discussions of WIL-knowledge that we will need to engage with – she will not be our main protagonist.

Instead, our main protagonist will be the relationship between two theses about WIL-knowledge (or, more precisely, schemas for generating putative necessary conditions for possessing specific instances of this knowledge):

> **The Experience Condition**: One knows what it is like to Φ only if one has had an experience of Φ-ing oneself.
> **The Answer Condition**: One knows what it is like to Φ only if one knows an answer to the question 'What is it like to Φ?'

These theses are both related to central themes in existing discussions of WIL-knowledge. The experience condition is simply a way of generalising a kind of powerful intuition that you cannot know what it is like to do or be something until you have done or been that thing oneself. This is the intuition that supports the standard assumption that Mary cannot know what it is like to see something red until that fateful day that she sees something red herself, and this intuition is prominent in most of the other applied discussions of WIL-knowledge (e.g., it plays a crucial role in characterising Paul's notion of a transformative experience). But it is also an intuition found in everyday and non-philosophical contexts, including numerous pop songs, like Smokey Robinson's 'You Don't Know What It's Like' where he sings "Til you fall until it happens to you. Oh, no, no, no, you don't know what it's like".[1]

The answer condition is supported by plausible ideas that were identified as far back as Ginet (1975), although it took a long time for these ideas to be more widely accepted in the literature on the knowledge argument, due to the work of Lycan (1996: 92–94) and others. These ideas can be stated both in the formal mode as claims about the structure and semantics of knowing-WIL ascriptions and by parallel claims, in the material mode, about the conditions in which someone knows what it is like to Φ. In short, knowing-WIL appears to be a form of so-called *knowing-wh*, and the sentences ascribing knowing-WIL appear to be knowing-wh ascriptions. The term 'knowing-wh' refers to any form of knowledge ascribed by sentences where the compliment of 'knows' is an interrogative clause denoting an embedded question and headed by a question word like 'why', 'when', 'where', 'what', 'whom', or 'how' (as most of these question words start with 'wh' we get the slightly awkward phrase 'knowing-wh'). And the standard question-answer semantics for knowing-wh ascriptions is, roughly, that they are true just in case the subject knows a relevant answer to the given embedded question. In which case, as knowing-WIL is a form of knowing-wh, we should expect that knowing-WIL is also analysable in terms of knowing an answer to an embedded question.

While strong prima facie cases can be made for both the experience and answer conditions, there is also a prima facie tension between these theses, as they seem to push us towards inconsistent views of WIL-knowledge. To be clear, there is *not* an inconsistency between these theses, and we will see later that some theorists have offered views of WIL-knowledge that entail both theses. However, there is still an apparent tension between endorsing both theses because accepting each thesis seems to push us towards accepting one of two different, and mutually inconsistent, views of WIL-knowledge.

---

[1] See Kind (2021) and Stoljar (2016) for similar examples.

On the one hand, the answer condition clearly pushes us towards an 'intellectualist' view on which knowing-WIL is a kind of propositional knowledge or 'knowing-that', that is, the knowledge you have when you know *that* something is the case. This is because knowing an answer to a question is naturally analysed as a matter of knowing that p, for some proposition p which is an answer to that question. In which case, it is hard to accept the answer condition without granting that WIL-knowledge can be at least partly analysed in terms of propositional knowledge. And once one accepts the answer condition one might naturally take a further step and claim that WIL-knowledge can be fully analysed in terms of propositional knowledge, such that knowing a propositional answer to the relevant embedded question is not just a necessary but a sufficient condition for possessing WIL-knowledge. In other words, once one accepts the answer condition it might seem natural to also endorse the following biconditional: one knows what it is like to Φ if and only if one knows an answer to the question 'What is it like to Φ?' In which case, WIL-knowledge would be a straightforward instance of propositional knowledge.

On the other hand, however, the experience condition might seem to push us towards an 'anti-intellectualist' view on which knowing-WIL is some form of non-propositional knowledge. For if WIL-knowledge was propositional knowledge *about* experiences why would possessing that knowledge entail one's having had an instance of the very thing that is the intentional object of one's knowledge? (I know that houses are overly priced, but, sadly, possessing this knowledge does not entail that I have ever had an overpriced house.) This entailment would make sense if knowing what it is like to Φ was a matter of knowing a proposition that entails that one has had an experience of Φ-ing at some point. For, given the factivity of knowledge-that, it would thereby follow that one has had an experience of Φ-ing. But, as we will see later in Section 3.1, intellectualist analyses of WIL-knowledge do not appeal to such propositional contents. The contents they appeal to might entail conditionals like *if* the subject of the knowing-WIL ascription were to have an experience of Φ-ing *then* it would feel a certain way for them, but they do not entail that the subject has had such an experience. So, why would the experience condition be true if knowing-WIL is just a matter of knowing such a proposition?

More generally, one might worry that in being subject to the experience condition the properties of WIL-knowledge will diverge in significant ways from those of knowledge-that. So, for example, consider testimony. Knowing-that, and many forms of knowing-wh other than knowing-WIL, can usually be shared via testimony (Poston 2016), at least in suitably favourable circumstances. But is WIL-knowledge transmissible through testimony? If the experience condition is true, it seems not, as while testimony might transmit knowledge it cannot transmit *experiences*. If you have just returned from a visit to the pyramids no amount of reliable testimony from you about what it was like will magically provide me with that experience.

My aim in this Element is to show how we can illuminate the nature of WIL-knowledge by exploring and, ultimately, resolving this tension between the experience and answer conditions. For, as we will see, the apparent tension between these theses is at the heart of various key issues concerning WIL-knowledge, including whether it can be analysed in terms of other forms of knowledge and the possible sources of this knowledge. In Sections 2 and 3, I will consider two broadly different ways that one might respond to the apparent tension between these theses that each appeal to two importantly different views of WIL-knowledge found in the literature. The first family of views, discussed in Section 2, are those which take WIL-knowledge to be some kind of non-propositional knowledge. Specifically, we will consider the *ability hypothesis* and the *acquaintance hypothesis* which respectively identify WIL-knowledge with non-propositional knowing-how and acquaintance knowledge. The second family of views, discussed in Section 3, are what I will call *qualified intellectualist* views as these views hold that knowing-WIL is a kind of knowing-that, but a distinctive species of knowing-that which is subject to some further condition beyond just knowing an answer to the embedded WIL-question.

Our discussion in Section 2 will show that the ability hypothesis and the acquaintance hypothesis can, at best, only provide us with an analysis of the epistemic states denoted by one of two different disambiguations of knowing-WIL sentences, and they cannot resolve the tension between the experience and answer conditions. Our discussion in Section 3 will show how qualified intellectualism can give us an account of the epistemic states denoted by the other disambiguation, and in Section 4 I will develop my own preferred form of qualified intellectualism – what I call downstream intellectualism – which can resolve this tension, and in a non-ad hoc way appealing to general patterns in how we think about and ascribe knowing-wh. In Section 5 these ideas are refined again to show how WIL-knowledge can come in degrees, which will help us to resolve certain puzzling conflicts in our attitudes and practices concerning WIL-knowledge and testimony which relate to the tension between the experience and answer conditions. One of the ideas to come out of that discussion will be that we can gain certain forms of partial WIL-knowledge about experiences we have not had ourselves, including the experiences of other people whose lives may be very different from one's own life. In Section 6 I will close by considering certain objections, both epistemological and ethical, that might be made to that idea.

2 Anti-Intellectualism

One way to react to the apparent tension between the experience and answer conditions would be to simply reject the answer condition by appealing to a view on which WIL-knowledge is some form of non-propositional knowledge, whilst maintaining that the experience condition is true and appealing to certain characteristics of this non-propositional knowledge to explain why it is true.

But what kind of knowledge could WIL-knowledge be if not a kind of knowledge-that? In textbooks one often finds the claim that as well as (i) knowing-that (or 'propositional knowledge'), there is also (ii) knowing-how, and (iii) acquaintance knowledge. Knowing-how is sometimes called 'ability knowledge' because following Ryle (1949) it is often assumed that to know how to Φ is to possess an ability or disposition to Φ. The term 'acquaintance knowledge' is sometimes used interchangeably with 'objectual knowledge' because the supposed examples of acquaintance knowledge are all cases where what one knows is a thing or object of some kind. But, for clarity, I will use these terms differently. I will use 'objectual knowledge' to refer to any form of knowledge where what one knows is an object of some kind (e.g., 'Mary knows Tokyo', 'Mary knows Fred', or 'Mary knows the experience of seeing something red') with no further assumptions made about the nature of this knowledge, for example, whether it can or cannot be analysed in terms of knowing-that. And I will reserve the term 'acquaintance knowledge' to refer to those supposed forms of objectual knowledge which also meet at least some of the substantive conditions associated with Russel's (1911) famous account of knowledge by acquaintance; including the negative claim that acquaintance knowledge is not a form of knowing-that, and the positive claim that it involves some kind of direct awareness of the known object (for discussion see Duncan 2021).

The standard story in the textbooks is that Ryle taught us that knowing-how is not reducible to knowing-that, and Russell taught us the same with respect to acquaintance knowledge, and there is clearly an implicit assumption that knowing-that could not be reducible to either knowing-how or acquaintance knowledge. So, if this standard picture is right, these are three mutually irreducible forms of knowledge. This tripartite picture can be challenged in lots of ways, and even if it is correct there are difficult questions about how to best interpret and develop it (e.g., what, if anything, unifies these three things such that we can consider them as all being different species of one overarching category of 'knowledge'?). But, for the moment, let us put such questions to the side, and assume that this standard picture is correct. Can we plausibly identify WIL-knowledge with either knowing-how or acquaintance knowledge?

2.1 The Ability and Acquaintance Hypotheses

Both identifications have been tried in the knowledge argument literature, with the hope being that one could thereby block the argument's crucial assumption that if Mary gains new WIL-knowledge then she must thereby come to know a new fact. Perhaps most famously, there is Lewis (1988) and Nemirow's (1990) respective versions of *the ability hypothesis* according to which knowing what it is like to Φ is identified with knowing-how. So, for example, Lewis holds that knowing what it is like to Φ is a matter of knowing how to imagine, remember, and recognise experiences of Φ -ing. Nemirow has the same kind of view, but he only appeals to the ability to imagine: 'Knowing what an experience is like is the same as knowing how to imagine having the experience' (1990: 495).

Furthermore, Lewis and Nemirow implicitly endorse a Rylean view of knowing-how on which knowing how to Φ is identified with the ability to Φ, *and* it is also assumed that this means that knowing-how is not identical to, and does not, in any other way, involve the possession of any states of knowing-that. Putting these points together, and using Lewis' set of abilities, we can usefully represent the ability hypothesis as being composed of three claims where the final claim follows from the first two claims:

i) To know what it is like to Φ is to know how to imagine, remember, and recognise, experiences of Φ-ing.
ii) To know how to imagine, remember, and recognise, experiences of Φ-ing is to have abilities to imagine, remember, and recognise, experiences of Φ-ing, abilities which do not involve the possession of any form of knowing-that.
iii) Knowing what it is like to Φ does not involve the possession of any form of knowing-that [from (i) and (ii)]

If this view is correct then we should reject the answer condition because WIL-knowledge is not a matter of knowing propositions at all and, hence, it cannot require knowing a proposition that answers a question. With regard to the experience condition, Lewis would reject this thesis as stated, as he thought that it was at least metaphysically possible to have the abilities to imagine and recognise experiences of Φ-ing without ever having Φ-ed oneself. But Lewis did think that, normally, one would need to have had an experience of Φ-ing in order to have the abilities to imagine, remember, and recognise experiences of Φ-ing, and Lewis could appeal to this idea in explaining the intuitive appeal of the experience condition, and he could even claim that it explains why a modified version of the experience restricted to 'normal circumstances' is true (we will explore Lewis' views more fully in Section 4.2).

In line with the tripartite picture of knowledge, the other strategy if one wants to reject the answer condition and deny that knowing-WIL is any kind of knowing-that is to identify it with some form of direct acquaintance knowledge, and then to claim, in addition, that possessing acquaintance knowledge is not a matter of possessing any form of knowledge-that. More precisely, this view will endorse some version of the following three claims paralleling aforementioned (i)–(iii):

(iv) To know what it is like to Φ is to possess a form of acquaintance knowledge.
 (v) Possessing this form of acquaintance knowledge is a matter of standing in a certain direct awareness relation to one's own experiences of Φ-ing, a relation which does not involve the possession of any form of knowing-that.
(vi) Knowing what it is like to Φ does not involve the possession of any form of knowing-that [from (i) and (ii)]

In the knowledge argument literature, Conee (1994) offered an *acquaintance hypothesis* like this, where he endorses each of (iv)–(vi). Conee holds, broadly following the tripartite picture and Russell (1911), that acquaintance knowledge requires neither information nor abilities and, hence, is 'irreducible to factual knowledge or knowing how' (1994: 136). On Conee's view, knowing what it is like to, say, see something red is a matter of being directly acquainted with an experience of seeing something red (which he treats as equivalent to becoming directly acquainted with the property of phenomenal redness). And being directly acquainted with an experience is, for Conee, simply a matter of having the experience and noticing it. If correct, this view of Conee's entails both that the experience condition is true (because one cannot know an experience in the way Conee describes without having an experience of that type) and that the answer condition is false (because this acquaintance knowledge is non-propositional knowledge).

2.2 Propositional Objections and the Ambiguity Reply

The ability hypothesis has been subjected to intense scrutiny, with numerous objections being made to it, including: arguments that Lewis' abilities are not sufficient (Conee 1994) or not necessary for the possession of WIL-knowledge (Conee 1994; Tye 2000), objections that contest its assumption that knowing-how is not a kind of knowing-that (Stanley and Williamson 2001), objections that contest the assumption that knowing-how can be identified with abilities (Alter 2001), and objections that contest the assumption that Lewis' abilities would not involve the possession of propositional knowledge (Coleman 2009).

Most importantly, for our purposes, there are also objections based on direct arguments that knowing-WIL is a form of knowing-that (e.g., Ginet 1975; Lycan 1996). These arguments appeal to the same kinds of considerations which support the answer condition, namely, that knowing-WIL ascriptions are a form of knowing-wh ascription, and that knowing-wh ascriptions are naturally analysed in terms of propositional knowledge where one knows a proposition that answers the embedded *wh*-question. And if any one of these arguments is sound, then we must also reject the acquaintance hypothesis (which has not been subjected to the same levels of intense scrutiny as the ability hypothesis), given that both hypotheses share the anti-intellectualist commitment that knowing-WIL is not any kind of propositional knowledge (claims iii/vi in Section 2.1).

In response, anti-intellectualists about WIL-knowledge could try to argue that there is no good sense at all in which we can say that WIL-knowledge is a kind of knowing-that. But I think the prospects for that kind of reply are dim, given the strength of the reasons supporting the answer condition. Another, and more promising, strategy would be to concede that these arguments provide us with good reasons to think that the epistemic states denoted by *one* disambiguation of knowing-WIL sentences are a kind of knowing-that, but then claim that there is *another* disambiguation which denotes a non-propositional form of knowledge.

This kind of reply can appeal to the plausible linguistic claim, following Stoljar (2015; 2016), that knowing-WIL ascriptions like 'John knows what it is like to have a toothache' are ambiguous between: (i) an *interrogative reading* on which the sentence tells us that John knows that *p* for some proposition *p* that answers the embedded question 'what is it like to have a toothache', and (ii) a *free relative reading* on which the sentence tells us that John knows the thing or property denoted by the referring expression 'what it is like to have a toothache'. As Stoljar (2016: 1182–1183) points out, the interrogative reading is used when we say things like 'I wonder what it is like to have a toothache' as what you are wondering is what true proposition or fact answers a question. And the free relative reading is used when we say things like, 'John hates what it is like to have a toothache' because what John hates is something like the way it feels to have a toothache, not a proposition that answers a question.

The free-relative interpretation obviously fits very naturally with the acquaintance hypothesis, because Conee can claim that on the free relative interpretation of 'John knows what it is like to have a toothache' what the sentence says is that John knows a certain experience or phenomenal quality, rather than any proposition that answers a question about that experience. Conee could then qualify his acquaintance hypothesis and claim that it is a view just about the kind of knowledge ascribed by the free relative interpretation of knowing-WIL ascriptions. In which case, Conee could plausibly maintain that the standard arguments for thinking that knowing-WIL is a form of knowing-that only apply to the interrogative reading of knowing-WIL ascriptions, and so they don't conflict with this ambiguity version of his acquaintance hypothesis.

Conee's reply to the knowledge argument would then be reformulated along similar lines. In Conee's original reply he agrees with Jackson that, before her release, Mary does not know what it is like to see something red, and after her release she gains this knowledge. But in learning what it is like to see something red Conee claims that Mary does not thereby come to know any new fact because WIL-knowledge is non-propositional acquaintance knowledge. Now if Conee were to accept that there is both a free-relative and an interrogative reading of knowing-WIL ascriptions his modified view would be that Mary has interrogative WIL-knowledge before leaving her room, but only after she leaves her room does she gain this acquaintance WIL-knowledge. And this reformulation fits well with claims Conee makes about pre-release Mary being able to know certain demonstrative facts concerning phenomenal redness, as some of these facts will plausibly be answers to the question, 'what is it like to see something red?' Conee (1994: 142) writes:

> There are closely related facts, such as the fact concerning phenomenal redness that red things look *that* way. But we have no reason to doubt that Mary knew all such facts before knowing how red things look. Mary already had the capacity to form thoughts using this demonstrative sort of reference to phenomenal qualities. She was able to demonstrate them with comprehension, at least via others' experiences of them, e.g. as 'that look' while indicating another person's attentive experience of phenomenal redness.

In embracing the ambiguity thesis in this way, this reformulation of Conee's acquaintance hypothesis could sidestep any arguments for thinking that knowing-WIL is a kind of knowing-that, by claiming that they only show us that the interrogative WIL-knowledge Mary had prior to leaving her room is a kind of knowing-that.

More importantly, for our purposes, this ambiguity version of the acquaintance hypothesis could also be used to motivate an interesting response to the prima facie tension between the answer and experience conditions. Now instead of denying the answer condition outright the proponent of this version of the acquaintance hypothesis could maintain that: (i) the answer condition is true, but only when we interpret it using the interrogative readings of knowing-WIL ascriptions, whereas it is false when we interpret it using the free relative reading; and (ii) the experience condition is true, but only when we interpret it using the free relative reading of knowing-WIL ascriptions, whereas it is false when we interpret it using the interrogative reading. And this position would have the attractive virtue of allowing that there is something right about each condition, whilst also dissolving the prima facie tension between them.

Furthermore, and surprisingly, these benefits of the ambiguity thesis may even be available to proponents of the ability hypothesis. For Stoljar (2015) has argued that Lewis' version of the ability hypothesis is best interpreted as an account of the epistemic states denoted by the free-relative interpretation of knowing-WIL ascriptions. The initial idea then would be that we could still endorse claims (i)–(iii) that we used early in characterising the ability hypothesis, but on this free-relative interpretation they will be equivalent to the following claims:

i) To know the experience of Φ-ing is to know how to imagine, remember, and recognise, experiences of Φ-ing.
ii) To know how to imagine, remember, and recognise, experiences of Φ-ing is to have abilities to imagine, remember, and recognise, experiences of Φ-ing, abilities which do not involve the possession of any form of knowing-that.
iii) Knowing the experience of Φ-ing does not involve the possession of any form of knowing-that [from (i) and (ii)]

Although, as Stoljar discusses, given the arguments for thinking that knowing-how is a kind of knowing-that (Stanley and Williamson 2001), and the close parallels between those arguments and the direct arguments for thinking that knowing-WIL is a kind of knowing-that, a proponent of this ambiguity version of the ability hypothesis may well choose to remove any claims about knowing-how from their view, and just identify this objectual knowledge directly with abilities. In which case, we would be left with the following theses:

i) To know the experience of Φ-ing is to have abilities to imagine, remember, and recognise, experiences of Φ-ing, abilities which do not involve the possession of any form of knowing-that.
ii) Knowing the experience of Φ-ing does not involve the possession of any form of knowing-that [from (i)]

This interpretation of Lewis' ability hypothesis, combined with the ambiguity thesis about knowing-WIL ascriptions, can have the same payoffs as the proposed reformulation of Conee's view identified earlier. That is, Lewis can now simply sidestep the arguments for thinking that WIL-knowledge is a form of knowing-that, as well as the related arguments for thinking that knowing-how is a kind of knowing-that, and he can dissolve the tension between the answer and experience conditions by claiming that each condition is true on one disambiguation of 'S knows what it is like to Φ' ascriptions, but not the same disambiguation.

2.3 Objectual WIL-knowledge

My focus in Sections 3–5 will be on interrogative WIL-knowledge alone, partly because I take this to be the more dominant interpretation of knowing-WIL ascriptions and partly because, as I will argue in Section 2.4, the tension between the answer and experience conditions remains for interrogative WIL-knowledge even once we distinguish it from objectual WIL-knowledge. But, before moving on to this focus on interrogative WIL-knowledge, it will be useful to briefly consider the nature of objectual WIL-knowledge. Does either the acquaintance hypothesis or the ability hypothesis provide us with a plausible theory of these epistemic states ascribed by the free-relative interpretation of knowing-WIL sentences?

Interestingly, there is a view on which we can see both the acquaintance hypothesis and the ability hypothesis as providing us with part of the picture when it comes to analysing objectual WIL-knowledge. This idea relates to arguments made by Conee and others that Lewis' abilities are not necessary for the possession of WIL-knowledge. So, Conee (1994: 139) appeals to a variant of Jackson's thought experiment where the added wrinkle is that Mary 'has no visual imagination' and is thereby 'unable to visualize anything'. Now, consider *this* Mary when she sees something red for the first time. Conee claims that it is evident that at that moment she looks at the red tomato this Mary knows what it is like to see something red but '*A fortiori*, she is not able to imagine, remember, and recognize the experience, as Lewis' Ability Hypothesis requires' (1994: 139). Furthermore, Conee suggests that the moral of his version of the Mary case is that Mary could lack *all* three of Lewis' abilities whilst still knowing what it is like to see something red. For Conee thinks that what this Mary case shows is 'that knowing what an experience is like requires nothing more than noticing the experience as it is undergone' and, hence, requires 'no ability to do anything other than to notice an experience' (1994: 139).

In response, Nemirow (2006: 35) suggests that in 'stripping [Mary] of all ability to imagine colour, Conee may have inadvertently denied her the knowledge at issue' on the grounds that when attributing knowledge of what it is like to see a red tomato 'to ordinary people who are staring at a red tomato, we assume that they can activate a panoply of imaginative abilities'. It is true that we make this assumption, as Conee acknowledges, as normally anyone who is knowing the experience of seeing a red tomato as they have that experience would also have the abilities Nemirow has in mind. But Conee's thought, I take it, is that this connection looks to be only a contingent connection, in which case we cannot *identify* knowing an experience with those abilities. And Nemirow's response doesn't seem to do much more than just point to the assumption that normally WIL-knowledge will be accompanied by such abilities, and so it is not clear that he has addressed Conee's objection.

At the heart of this dispute is, of course, Conee's assumption that there is this distinctive way of knowing an experience as one is having that very experience, which simply consists in having the experience and noticing it. And if Conee's argument against the ability hypothesis is on the right track then it seems that we cannot analyse that knowledge in terms of the possession of abilities to imagine, remember, and recognise experiences of that type. However, as Conee himself discusses (1994: 139), his view is consistent with the idea that such abilities could be involved in knowing an experience after the experience has ended. In which case, we could see the acquaintance hypothesis as providing us with the correct account of the distinctive objectual WIL-knowledge one can possess as one is having an experience, and the ability hypothesis as providing us with the correct account of the objectual WIL-knowledge one can possess after the experience has ended.

Of course, a proponent of the ability hypothesis would surely reject this split view of the conditions needed to possess objectual WIL-knowledge. They might argue, for example, that Conee is simply confusing properties of our experiences themselves – that they are a kind of event and so cannot be identified with abilities as those are a kind of standing state as opposed to an event – with properties of our knowledge of those experiences as they occur. So, a proponent of the ability hypothesis might well grant to Conee the, in principle, possibility of cases where someone has an *experience* without possessing any of Lewis' abilities, but they will maintain that in such a scenario one would not know what it is like to have that experience; and then they could try to argue that any inclination we have to think otherwise is a confusion stemming from the fact that normally the experience would always be accompanied by this knowledge.

More could be said on these topics. But for my purposes we need not investigate these issues further here, given that I want to focus on interrogative WIL-knowledge. In the remaining discussion, I will simply take it as a working assumption that objectual WIL-knowledge cannot be reductively analysed as a species of propositional knowledge, and that its correct analysis will be one that analyses it at least partly in terms of either acquaintance and/or ability knowledge.

2.4 Limitations of the Ambiguity Reply

The acquaintance and ability hypotheses might be plausible when we restrict them to the objectual interpretation of knowing-WIL sentences, and as just discussed there may even be a sense in which both accounts can provide us with partially correct analyses of objectual WIL-knowledge. Furthermore, as we saw in Section 2.2, the ambiguity versions of these hypotheses have some initially attractive features insofar as they enable one to sidestep arguments for the conclusion that knowing-WIL is a kind of knowing-that, and one can appeal to the ambiguity thesis to defuse the apparent tension between the experience and answer conditions. However, on closer inspection, I think that, for related reasons, the ambiguity versions of these hypotheses cannot provide us with either a good reply to the knowledge argument, or a good way of dissolving the tension between the experience and answer conditions.

The problem with respect to the knowledge argument is that it is not plausible that Mary would *only* gain objectual WIL-knowledge, and not any propositional WIL-knowledge. When Mary sees something red for the first time Conee acknowledges that she will make 'an exciting discovery. "Aha!", she might well exclaim' (1994: 139), but Conee holds, of course, that this discovery will consist solely in her becoming acquainted with the property of phenomenal redness. However, as well as exclaiming, 'Aha!' Mary might also say to herself, 'I always wondered what it is like to see something red, and now I know!' But the use of 'wondered' here forces the interrogative reading of 'what it is like' (Stoljar 2016) because wondering is a relation to a question. What Mary wonders is what the *answer* might be to the question, 'what is it like to see something red?' indicating that when Mary becomes acquainted with phenomenal redness for the first time, she not only comes to know that property itself, but she also comes to know a new fact *about* that property (that *this* is what it is like to see something red) which answers the question that was the object of her wondering prior to leaving her room.

As noted in Section 2.2, Conee seems to think that any such demonstrative knowledge-that is knowledge Mary could already have possessed before leaving her room, on the grounds that she could demonstratively refer to phenomenal redness in other ways (e.g., by demonstrating the attentive experiences of another person). But, as Tye (2011: 306) discusses in relation to similar cases, the state of demonstrative knowledge that pre-release Mary has when she knows that *that* [demonstrating the occurrent experience of another person] is what it is like to see something red is, intuitively, different from the state of demonstrative knowledge that post-release Mary has when she knows that *that* [demonstrating her own occurrent experience] is what it is like to see something red. How exactly to account for this difference is, of course, a difficult matter (e.g., whether to account for it in terms of different demonstrative concepts of some kind, or the same concept but still a different type of knowledge-that), and we will touch on these issues in Section 3.2. But we shouldn't let that difficulty obscure the point that, intuitively, these are two very different states of knowledge.

Related issues undermine the ambiguity strategy for defusing the tension between the experience and answer conditions. The problem with this strategy is that it is not plausible that the intuitive case for the experience condition only applies to the objectual knowledge ascribed by the free-relative interpretation of knowing-WIL ascriptions, and not the propositional form of knowledge ascribed by the interrogative interpretation. For the natural explanation of why Mary does not possess the relevant demonstrative knowledge-that prior to leaving her room is that she has not yet had an experience of seeing something red, which suggests that *interrogative* WIL-knowledge is subject to an experience condition. And, yet, knowing what it is like to see something red (in the interrogative sense) is a matter of knowing that p for some proposition p that answers the question 'what is it like to see something red?' So, the prima facie tension between the experience and answer conditions remains for the form of knowledge ascribed by the interrogative interpretation of knowing-WIL ascriptions.

3 Qualified Intellectualism

Turning to the epistemic states denoted by the interrogative interpretation of knowing-WIL sentences it seems undeniable (once we acknowledge that there *is* such an interpretation) that we should endorse the intellectualist view that these are states of knowing-that, where the known proposition answers the relevant embedded WIL-question. But if we embrace the answer condition like this, what are we to do about this remaining tension with the experience condition?

One approach would be to argue that we should reject the experience condition outright for the interrogative interpretation of knowing-WIL sentences, thereby endorsing the mirror image to what proponents of non-propositional views of WIL-knowledge might try to say in response to the apparent tension between these two theses. In due course we will consider reasons for weakening and qualifying the experience condition in different ways but even then, we will still be able to acknowledge that there are important truths in the vicinity of this idea that interrogative WIL-knowledge is subject to an experience condition. And that is important, because as we have just seen, the intuitions expressed by the experience condition arise for interrogative WIL-knowledge and not just objectual WIL-knowledge. (Please note that from here on any unqualified uses of 'WIL-knowledge' and 'knowing-WIL', should be taken as referring to interrogative WIL-knowledge.)

Fortunately, rejecting the experience condition outright is not the only response that an intellectualist can make to this tension between the experience and answer conditions. Another strategy is to claim that knowing what it is like to Φ is not merely a matter of knowing some proposition which answers the embedded WIL-question, but also satisfying some further condition which explains why the experience condition is true, or at least why this principle is intuitively appealing. So, on this kind of view WIL-knowledge is a species of knowing-that but a distinctive species of it which involves the satisfaction of this further condition. This strategy relies on the fact that the answer condition only tells us that knowing an answer to the embedded WIL-question is a necessary condition for possessing WIL-knowledge, not that it is both a necessary and a sufficient condition.

I think this kind of qualified intellectualism provides us with the best view of interrogative WIL-knowledge. But there are notable issues that this broad kind of view needs to address. One obvious set of issues concerns just what exact form of qualified intellectualism we should endorse, including what kinds of propositions are thought to answer embedded WIL-questions, and what further condition exactly will be added to the analysis of WIL-knowledge. Another important, but I think overlooked, issue is how to address the following concern one could have with qualified intellectualism: Why isn't adding some kind of further condition to our analysis of WIL-knowledge not just an ad hoc solution to the problem of analysing this form of knowledge and addressing the tension between the experience and the answer conditions? In this section I will consider how the qualified intellectualist position might be developed so that it addresses the first set of issues, and then in the next section I will offer my on preferred form of qualified intellectualism that can also address the ad hoc concern.

3.1 The Contents of WIL-Knowledge

What kinds of propositions does one know when one knows what it is like to Φ? A number of views have been suggested, but, for reasons of space, I will focus on just explaining some of the key details of what I take to be the most plausible and well-developed theory, namely, Stoljar's (2016) affective theory of 'what it is like' expressions (including but not limited to knowing-WIL sentences). To help introduce and motivate this view it will be useful to consider how some other forms of knowing-wh are standardly analysed. For example, if we take knowing-where, knowing-why, and knowing-how ascriptions it is often suggested that these ascriptions respectively quantify over *locations*, *reasons*, and *ways* of performing actions. So, consider the following sentences:

(1a) Hannah knows where Bill is.
(1b) Hannah knows why Bill left the party.
(1c) Hannah knows how to ride a bike.
(1d) Hannah knows what it is like to ride a bike.

A standard application of the question-answer semantics for knowing-wh[2] would give the something like the following truth conditions for sentences (1a)–(1c):

(1a*) 'Hannah knows where Bill is' is true in a context c if and only if, in c, there is some location l such that Hannah knows that Bill is at l.
(1b*) 'Hannah knows why Bill left the party' is true in a context c if and only if, in c, there is some reason r such that Hannah knows that r is the reason Bill left the party.
(1c*) 'Hannah knows how to ride a bike' is true in a context c if and only if, in c, there is some way w such that Hannah knows that w is a way for her to ride a bike.

Stoljar (2016: 1169–1170) thinks there are close connections between knowing-WIL ascriptions like (1d) and other knowing-wh ascriptions like (1a)–(1c), and especially knowing-how ascriptions like (1c), as indicated by the fact that 'what is it like' questions can be very close in meaning to 'how' questions. And, in line with those connections, Stoljar suggests that knowing-how and knowing-WIL ascriptions both quantify over *ways*, with knowing-how ascriptions quantifying over *ways of performing actions*, and knowing-WIL ascriptions quantifying over *ways of being affected by events*. More specifically, Stoljar's theory gives us the following truth conditions for a sentence like (1d):

(1d*) 'Hannah knows what it is like to ride a bike' is true in a context c if and only if, in c, there is some way w such that Hannah knows that y's bike riding affects x in way w.

There are two key elements in Stoljar's theory: (i) the idea that WIL-sentences express *affective relations* between subjects and events, and (ii) the claim that there are two subject positions – one for an agent of the event, and one for an experiencer of the event – in the logical form of the embedded question.

---

[2] For simplicity I am just focusing here on the more dominant 'mention-some' reading of these sentences (where one merely needs to know one answer to the embedded question), rather than the 'mention all' reading (where one needs to know all its answers).

Affective relations are relations of an individual being affected in some way by the occurrence of an event, where the relevant sense of 'affect' is a 'modest' one on which 'it means something like "influence" or "bring about a change or condition in"' (Stoljar 2016: 1173). This modest notion of an affective relation helps Stoljar to explain the fact that we typically use WIL-sentences to talk about experiences, whilst still managing to accommodate certain non-experiential uses of WIL-sentences. Consider the following sentences:

(2a)   What has it been like for the UK to leave the EU?
(2b)   Mary knows what it has been like for the UK to leave the EU.

In many contexts, (2a) would be used to ask a question just about how the UK has been economically or politically affected by the event of leaving the EU, as opposed to, say, how the average UK citizen, or the UK as a collective, has been experientially affected by that event. In which case, in such contexts, if we were to assert (2b) we would only be attributing knowledge to Mary of some fact about how the UK has been economically or politically affected by its leaving of the EU.

Still, while WIL-sentences can be used to talk about non-experiential ways of being affected by an event, Stoljar maintains that the *stereotypical* use of such sentences is to talk about experiential ways of being affected by events, where this is a matter of an individual feeling a certain way in virtue of that event. On Stoljar's theory then in a stereotypical context c a sentence of the form 'There is something it is like to ride a bike' will be true if and only if there is, in c, some *experiential* way that y's event/act of riding a bike affects x.

This example can also be used to illustrate Stoljar's claim that the logical form of a WIL-expression contains two argument positions: the standard one generated by the covert pronoun in the infinitival 'to ride a bike' which identifies the agent of the event, and the further argument position Stoljar posits for the finite clause 'what it is like to ride a bike' which identifies the experiencer of the event. In most contexts these will naturally be interpreted as being one and the same subject. So, if you ask me 'Do you know what it is like to ride a bike?' and I respond by saying 'No' (as I have, in fact, never ridden a bike) I will usually be interpreted as either communicating that I don't know how *my* riding a bike would make *me* feel, or perhaps that I don't know how *one's* riding a bike makes *one* feel, but not that I don't know how, say, *my* riding a bike would make *Bob* feel, or how *Bob's* riding a bike would make *me* feel. However, in certain contexts, the actor and experiencer positions can come apart. So, you might be interested, for example, in knowing what it is like to me for my son to ride a bike (say, shortly after he has first learnt to do so), and I might tell you that 'it's nerve wracking!' or 'it's humbling' (thinking of my inability to do the same).

3.2 The Extra Condition

Stoljar's affective theory has the significant virtue of being able to give an account of WIL-sentences which explains their intimate connections with how we think and talk about experiences, whilst also being able to accommodate a range of different uses of these expressions including non-experiential uses and uses where the experiencer of the event and the subject of the event come apart.

However, a key limitation of the affective theory, which is also a limitation of all the main competitors to this theory, is that such views purport to offer necessary and sufficient conditions for possessing WIL-knowledge (or the truth of knowing-WIL ascriptions) but they only seem to provide us with at best a necessary and not sufficient condition. The problem is that there are many contexts where someone knows the right kind of answer to an embedded 'what it is like to Φ' question but, intuitively, does not know what it is like to Φ.

So, for example, Tye (2011) imagines pre-release Mary having access to a cerebroscope which allows her to see an image of the precise brain state that a person is in as they are having an experience of seeing something red, and which 'according to some physicalists, just is what it is like to see something red' (2011: 305). If we assume, for the sake of argument, that the relevant form of physicalism is correct, then Tye thinks pre-release Mary could know that *that* [demonstrating the brain state displayed on the cerebroscope] is the way it feels to see something red (I'm adjusting Tye's example slightly here to fit with Stoljar's semantics), and she would thereby know a proposition that answers the question 'what is it like to see something red?' but, intuitively, she still does not yet know what it is like to see something red, given that she has not yet had the experience of seeing something red.

There are also more humdrum cases with this structure. Imagine Hannah, who has never ridden a bike or even tried to ride a bike. Nonetheless, echoing Conee's ideas discussed in Section 2.2, Hannah might still know that it feels *that* way to ride a bike, where the demonstrative denotes the way it feels to ride a bike for some person riding a bike past Hannah, or the way it feels to ride a bike as described in a book that Hannah has read, and so on. But, given that Hannah has never experienced riding a bike herself, one might think, in line with the experience condition, that she still does know what it is like to ride a bike.

To better understand how an intellectualist about knowing-WIL might try to solve this problem it will be useful to compare it to the closely parallel, and better known, insufficiency problems that arise for intellectualist views of knowing-how. So, in their well-known defence of intellectualism about knowing-how (or, more specifically, knowing-how-to), Stanley and Williamson (2001) initially give (1c*) as the truth conditions for (1c), that is, they hold that knowing, for some way w, that w is a way one can ride a bike is both a necessary and sufficient condition for knowing how to ride a bike. However, as Stanley and Williamson discuss, the Hannah example looks to be an insufficiency counterexample to their analysis of the truth-conditions for 'S knows how to Φ' sentences. For, looking at the person riding a bike near her, Hannah can know that *that* way is a way for her to ride a bike. However, intuitively, Hannah does not know how to ride a bike, given that she has never even tried to ride a bike and, hence, lacks the ability.

To address this problem Stanley and Williamson suggest that we need to add a 'practical mode of presentation' condition to either the semantic truth conditions for 'S knows how to Φ' sentences themselves, or to the pragmatic conditions for making felicitous assertions of such sentences (in which case, it would be true but infelicitous, at least in certain contexts, to assert that Hannah knows how to ride a bike).[3] So, for example, if we added this condition to the truth conditions of (1c), the idea is that they will now look like this:

(1c**) 'Hannah knows how to ride a bike' is true in a context c if and only if, for some way w, Hannah knows, *under a practical mode of presentation,* that w is a way for her to ride a bike.

Stanley and Williamson do not say a lot about what practical modes of presentation are, relying instead on the claim that as we need some notion of modes of presentation more generally (e.g., to handle cases of de se knowledge) it is justifiable to posit their existence. However, crucially, Stanley and Williamson do tell us that knowing, under a practical mode of presentation, that w is way for oneself to ride a bike 'will entail the possession of certain complex dispositions' (2001: 429) which are surely dispositions connected in some way to the performance of successful actions of riding a bike and are dispositions which Hannah lacks.

Stanley and Williamson also tell us that practical mode of presentations can be thought of either as a constituent of a fine-grained 'Fregean' proposition, or

---

[3] A reviewer asks how the 'mention-all' reading I put aside earlier (fn.2) interacts with the insufficiency problem. It is a good question because there will be some insufficiency cases where the explanation of why a subject lacks some form of knowing-wh will be that the mention-all reading is at issue (e.g., I usually won't count as knowing who went to the meeting if all I know is that Stephanie was there). But that kind of move won't help here. One problem is that the 'mention-all' reading is implausible in most contexts where we ascribe knowing-how. Furthermore, even if for every way to swim, say, one knew the relevant proposition of the form 'w is a way to swim' the concern at issue here is that it seems possible to possess all that knowledge in a way that, intuitively, does not suffice for knowing how to swim (e.g., by reading a book). What these points suggest is that the insufficiency problem at issue here is to do with how we possess knowledge of an answer to an embedded question (or perhaps knowing the right 'fine-grained' answer, see discussion below), rather than how many answers we know.

as a special way of entertaining a coarse-grained 'Russellian' proposition in thought; where a coarse-grained proposition is just an ordered sequence of objects and properties, whereas a 'fine grained' proposition also contains something like Fregean senses. On the Fregean view, one could respond to the insufficiency problem by claiming that knowing the right *fine-grained* answer to an embedded 'how to Φ' question will entail knowing how to Φ (Stanley 2011, Pavese 2015). On the Russellian view, however, one grants that *mere* knowledge of any propositional answer to an embedded 'how to Φ' question does not entail knowing how to Φ, but knowing the right proposition, in the right way, does (Stanley and Williamson 2001). What both views have in common is that they try to address the insufficiency problem by identifying knowing how to Φ with a form of propositional knowledge (distinguished either by its content, or by the way in which one entertains that content) which entails the possession of certain relevant dispositions or abilities.

What might a similar reply to the insufficiency problem look like for the intellectualist about WIL-knowledge? Following the structure of Stanley and Williamson's view, we might use the notion of a 'knowing in a phenomenal way' condition and then offer the following reformulation of Stoljar's affective theory:

> 'S knows what it is like to Φ' is true in a stereotypical context *c* if and only if, for some way *w*, S knows, *in a phenomenal way*, that *y*'s Φ-ing feels a certain way *w* for *x*.

The phenomenal way of knowing condition here is stated as part of the semantic truth conditions of knowing-WIL ascriptions. However, like Stanley and Williamson, I can be neutral on whether this phenomenal way of knowing condition should be incorporated into the semantics of knowing-WIL ascriptions as earlier or, alternatively, whether it should only find a place in the pragmatics of such ascriptions, that is, as a condition on when it is conversationally appropriate to make a knowing-WIL ascription. But, for simplicity, I will often talk as if it is part of the truth conditions.

As with practical modes of presentation, this notion of a 'phenomenal way of knowing' should be understood as a placeholder notion which can then be filled out in different ways. But, roughly paralleling Stanley and Williamson's claimed entailment from knowing under a practical mode of presentation to possessing certain dispositions or abilities, one initial claim one might make about this condition is that knowing, in a phenomenal way, that *w* is a way it feels to Φ entails one's having had an experience of Φ-ing oneself. Alternatively, one could parallel the practical mode of presentation even more closely, and appeal to an entailment from knowing, in a phenomenal way, that w is a way it feels to Φ to having Lewis' abilities to imagine, remember, and recognise experiences of Φ-ing. I will develop that latter idea in Section 4.2 but for now I will focus on the former idea, as that is the one most often developed in the literature (e.g., Tye 2011).

So, the suggestion for now will be that the insufficiency cases for WIL-knowledge can be avoided because while Hannah can know that *that* way is a way it feels to ride a bike (or, more precisely, 'a way it feels to Hannah for her to ride a bike'), she does not know this proposition in a phenomenal way, as that would entail her having had an experience of Φ-ing, and she has not had such an experience. And one can also appeal to this condition to reconcile the tension between the answer and experience conditions. For knowing in a phenomenal way entails experience in line with the experience condition, but knowing-WIL is still at least partly a matter of knowing an answer to the embedded WIL-question in line with the answer condition.

However, beyond this bare entailment claim, what more can been said to fill out this notion of a phenomenal way of knowing? Following Tye (2011), one broad family of views we can identify here are views according to which knowing, *in a phenomenal way*, that w is a way it feels to Φ is a matter of (i) knowing that w is a way it feels to Φ, and (ii) this knowledge must be based on one's own direct acquaintance with w through one's own experience(s) of Φ-ing. But what is the relevant notion of 'being based on' here? One way of interpreting it would be appeal to special experience/acquaintance dependent *concepts* of the way it feels to Φ and require that one's knowledge of an answer to the 'what is it like to Φ' must involve such a concept. So, for example, Tye (2011: 313) endorses a view like this when he writes:

> To know what it is like to experience red, one needs to know that experiencing red is (phenomenally) like this, where the demonstrative concept at play in one's knowledge was introduced into one's mental economy via an act of attending to the relevant phenomenal character in one's own visual experience.

On Tye's view knowing what it is like to experience red is a kind of knowing-that, but one which is based in acquaintance knowledge in the sense that this knowledge-that involves a demonstrative concept that was formed via one's direct acquaintance with the phenomenal character of one's own visual experience. And Tye and Sainsbury (2012), develop an 'originalist' theory of concepts, on which concepts are distinguished partly by their origins, which allows them to further support this idea that the demonstrative concept Mary forms using the cerebroscope is a different concept from the demonstrative concept she forms when she sees something red for the first time.

More generally, many notions of 'phenomenal concepts' could be appealed to explain why knowing, in a phenomenal way, that w is a way it feels to Φ entails one having Φ-ed at some point. This is because phenomenal concepts are often assumed to be experience entailing. As Sundström (2011: 271) says: 'phenomenal concept theorists typically claim that phenomenal concepts are *experience-dependent* in the sense that, in order to possess a phenomenal concept of some conscious state S one needs to oneself have experienced S'.

There are also ways of developing the 'basing' idea without appealing to any notion of special concepts. Grzankowski and Tye (2019), for example, suggest that the relevant sense of 'basing' involved in possessing WIL-knowledge is the epistemic basing relation. Applying this idea to post-release Mary, Grzankowski and Tye claim that her knowing what it is like to see something red is not only a matter of her knowing the right proposition (as they think that pre-release Mary already knew all the same fine-grained propositions) but also 'Mary's *reason* for believing that this is an experience of red . . . is the fact that she is acquainted with red through her experience of it' (2019: 86).

4 Downstream Intellectualism

There are many ways then to develop the notion of a phenomenal way of knowing. But why isn't adding any such condition to our analysis of WIL-knowledge not just an ad hoc solution to the tension between the answer and experience conditions and the related insufficiency challenges faced by intellectualist accounts of WIL-knowledge? As noted in Section 1, knowledge-that more generally is not subject to any similar kind of experience condition, so why would this species of knowledge-that be (or at least appear to be) subject to such a condition? What I want to do in this section is, first, introduce some broader ideas concerning our concept of knowledge and knowledge ascribing practices, which I will then appeal to in developing an intellectualist view of WIL-knowledge that can reconcile the tension between the answer and experience conditions whilst also addressing these ad hoc concerns.

4.1 Clients and Downstream Knowledge

Craig (1990) famously advocated for a new approach to epistemological inquiry. Craig suggests that we start by identifying plausible hypotheses about the *function* of our concept of knowledge, and then seek to provide analyses of the concept of knowledge that would explain how that concept could serve that function (as opposed to what Craig takes to be standard method which is trying to provide an analysis of our concept of knowledge that fits with our intuitions about its extension and intension). Given the limits of what we can learn about our environment just using our own faculties of perception and reason, Craig thought that as *inquirers* we have a basic human interest in accessing the information that other people have gained via their perceptual and reasoning faculties, which generates an interest in identifying people who are reliable sources of information. And Craig's hypothesis is that the central function of our concept of knowledge is to serve our interests as inquirers in identifying reliable informants.

However, in an illuminating discussion, Hawley (2011) explored how our concept of knowledge – especially in relation to knowledge-how – can also be viewed as serving our interests as *clients* where, unlike the inquirer, the client seeks people with knowledge not because they want their information for themselves but because they want someone who can reliably perform certain actions connected to that information. On this perspective then the function of our concept of knowledge is to serve our basic human interests in identifying reliable *performers*, rather than reliable informants. So, as Hawley points out, when I seek someone who knows how to fix a leak it is often because I simply want someone who can reliably perform controlled and intentional actions of fixing leaks, not because I want to know how to fix a leak myself. For I might have this knowledge already but just not want to do the work myself, or I may simply have no interest in acquiring this knowledge.

Craig's talk of the function of a concept might seem elusive, and his own function hypothesis is supported by a controversial state of nature argument. But, without taking any position on Craig's approach to epistemology, I think Craig and Hawley's very different observations about the interests served by our knowledge ascribing practices point us towards two importantly different ways of thinking about what knowledge is, and the conditions that a subject must meet to possess knowledge. Specifically, in other work (Cath 2023), I suggested that the distinction between the inquirer and the client points us towards a distinction between what I call *upstream knowledge* versus *downstream knowledge*.

To help explain this distinction, it is useful to make the orthodox (but by no means universal) assumption that knowledge is a species of true belief, such that any state of knowledge is a state of true belief but one which has certain further properties which 'upgrade' it into a state of knowledge. Typically, when epistemologists try to analyse knowledge the further properties, or conditions, that they reach for are 'upstream' properties, in the sense that they are properties to do with the aetiology of the true belief state. As Hookway (2006: 105) says the 'features that have been taken to be characteristic of knowledge have been backward-looking'. So, for example, that the true belief was the output of a reliable belief forming process, or that it was not based on an inference from a justified but false premise, or that it was based on good evidence, and so on.

However, when we turn to knowing how to Φ it is more natural to look to 'downstream' conditions connected to whether the true belief state is a state that is a reliable guide to possible future actions of Φ-ing, which relates to the interests of the client.

If we focus in on a true belief that w is a way for oneself to Φ (the kind of content that features in intellectualist analyses) the idea is that a subject S has *upstream knowledge* that w is a way for S to Φ just in case they have a true belief that w is a way for S to Φ, *and* this state of true belief has whatever upstream properties feature in one's preferred analysis of knowledge. On the other hand, a subject S has *downstream knowledge* that w is a way for S to Φ just in case they have a true belief that w is a way for S to Φ, and this true belief state has further downstream action-guiding properties such that S' being in this true belief state will entail and explain S' having a reliable ability to intentionally Φ in normal circumstances. And one can then plug in any existing account of how a true belief state could entail that one has such an ability, including views which appeal to different notions of practical modes of presentation (Stanley 2011; Pavese 2015), and accounts which appeal to practical ways of being in a propositional attitude state (Waights Hickman 2019; Cath 2020).

The hypothesis then is that 'S knows how to Φ' ascriptions are often, and stereotypically, used to attribute states of downstream knowledge to people. Note that this hypothesis is intentionally neutral on the semantic value of 'knows' in 'S knows how to Φ' ascriptions. It could be, for example, that in stereotypical contexts the semantic value is downstream knowledge and in other contexts it is upstream knowledge. But it could equally be that it is always one or the other epistemic state, and that when 'S knows how to Φ' ascriptions are used to attribute the other state this is achieved via pragmatics rather than the semantic meaning of the sentence. I will not take a stance on these options here. But if this use hypothesis is true then I think there is a good informal sense in which we can say that knowing-how is a form of downstream knowledge (the more precise claim being that one of the epistemic states that we use knowing-how ascriptions to identify is a form of downstream knowledge).

More importantly, intuitions about various hypothetical cases that feature heavily in debates about the nature of knowing-how can be usefully illuminated using this hypothesis. These include the *insufficiency cases* we discussed in Section 3.2, but also *redundancy cases* which arguably show that knowing-that (as normally conceived) is not necessary for knowing-how. This is because in these redundancy scenarios knowing-how is intuitively present despite a standard condition on knowing-that not being met, like one's true belief not being a 'Gettierized' true belief (Poston 2009; Cath 2011), or one's true belief being a doxastically justified true belief (Cath 2011; Carter and Navarro 2017).

With regard to the insufficiency cases, part of the explanation of why someone like Hannah intuitively fails to know how to ride a bike relies on the point that her true belief that *that* way [demonstrating the way that someone else riding a bike] is a way for her to ride a bike at best only constitutes downstream, and not upstream, knowledge, given that her possession of this true belief does not entail her having an ability to ride a bike intentionally in normal circumstances. And then, given the hypothesis that knowing-how ascriptions are paradigmatically used to attribute downstream knowledge, we can explain our intuition that Hannah lacks knowledge-how in terms of a kind of default expectation that someone who knows how to ride a bike will possess the relevant downstream knowledge and, consequently, will be able to ride a bike in normal circumstances.

With regard to the redundancy cases, these are explained by the fact that the relevant kinds of etiological properties that are absent in these cases – being a non-accidentally true belief or being a doxastically justified belief – are irrelevant to whether it is a state that can reliably guide actions of Φ-ing.

As just described, this upstream/downstream distinction only applies to the kind of propositional true beliefs involved in knowing how to Φ. But there are good reasons to think that the distinction will apply to propositional knowledge much more broadly. As Hawley (2011: 288–289) discusses, there are redundancy cases for other forms of knowing-wh where, intuitively, someone possesses knowing-wh even though their relevant true belief is a Gettierised true belief. And, in these cases, one could offer a parallel explanation to that for knowing-how of why this intuition is correct using the hypothesis that the relevant epistemic state is a form of downstream knowledge.

There are also insufficiency cases for other forms of knowing-wh. Consider James who has a true belief that the City Basement bookshop is on Flinders Street, but he has no ability to locate that bookshop when in the Melbourne CBD as this proposition is essentially all he knows about the location of the bookshop, and he is otherwise totally unfamiliar with the CBD area, and so on. Finding yourself lost with James it would be natural to say, 'you don't know where the bookshop is' or to criticise James if he had previously claimed to know where the bookshop is, and so on. And, again, the assumption that knowing-wh ascriptions are often used to identify people who possess downstream true beliefs can explain our intuitions about these insufficiency cases, as James' true belief is not one that will enable him to reliably perform successful actions of locating the bookshop. In which case, while James' true belief might constitute upstream knowledge (if it has the relevant upstream properties) it is, by definition, not a state of downstream knowledge.

4.2 Knowing-WIL as Downstream Knowledge

But what about knowing-WIL? Can the client's perspective and the idea of downstream knowledge illuminate the insufficiency cases we find for WIL-knowledge, and the related tensions between the answer and experience conditions? Here one might think that there is a big disanalogy between the factors that generate the insufficiency cases for other forms of knowing-wh and the factors that generate the insufficiency cases for knowing-WIL.

After all, the reason mere knowing-that seems to be insufficient for knowing how to Φ is that knowing-how entails some kind of ability condition. But the reason mere knowing-that seems to be insufficient for knowing what it is like to Φ is meant to be that this knowledge entails the possession of an *experience*, not an ability. However, I think this disanalogy is superficial because we can provide a deeper explanation of why mere knowing-that is insufficient for knowing-WIL in terms of the client's perspective and the hypothesis that knowing-WIL ascriptions are used to track a form of downstream knowledge.

To see how Hawley's perspective of the client can relate to WIL-knowledge recall Lewis' abilities to imagine, recognise, and remember experiences of Φ-ing. Now imagine a head chef who wants to choose one of her staff to replace her while she takes a holiday. In selecting someone for this role one of the things this chef will be interested in is identifying a person who possesses various forms of WIL-knowledge and the related abilities to imagine, recognise, and remember the way various experiences feel. So, for example, they will want someone who recognises what it is like to taste a dish which has too much salt, too little, or just the right amount. And the head chef will want someone who can imagine what it would be like if you added more umami flavouring to a dish, can recognise when their version of a dish tastes like the one made by the head chef, and can remember what the head chef's version of that dish tasted like, and so on. In seeking someone with these forms of WIL-knowledge and their associated abilities, the head chef is *not* in the situation of Craig's inquirer or apprentice (1990: 156) who is trying to acquire knowledge or skills for themselves, as they already possess these forms of knowledge and skills. Rather, the head chef is in the client's situation, as they are seeking someone who has certain forms of knowledge that will support that person in reliably performing associated actions for the client.

A qualified intellectualist needs to reject either Lewis' identification of knowing-WIL with the abilities to imagine, remember, and recognise, or his assumption that these abilities do not involve the possession of any propositional knowledge. But either way a qualified intellectualist can allow that knowing what it is like to Φ is closely connected to, and even entails, the possession of such abilities. Furthermore, they can endorse the following hypothesis about our uses of knowing-WIL ascriptions paralleling the one about knowing-how given in the previous section: 'S knows what it like to Φ' ascriptions are often, and stereotypically, used to attribute relevant states of downstream knowledge. So, the idea is that when we make a 'S knows what it like to Φ' ascription we are usually interested in identifying someone who not only has a true belief about the way it feels to Φ, but who possesses that true belief in such a way that they thereby possess certain relevant abilities, which following Lewis we can take to be abilities of imagining, recognising, and remembering experiences of Φ-ing.

This idea can help us to explain: (i) why WIL-knowledge is subject to insufficiency cases where someone knows a proposition that addresses the relevant embedded WIL-question but, intuitively, does not know what it is like to Φ; (ii) why, in normal circumstances, WIL-knowledge is subject to a qualified experience condition; and (iii) why adding this version of a phenomenal way of knowing condition to our intellectualist analysis is not just an ad hoc response to these insufficiency cases and the tension between the answer and experience conditions.

The explanation of (i) is that mere knowledge-that concerning the way it feels to Φ need not suffice for one to have any relevant abilities to imagine, recognise, and remember experiences of Φ-ing. We will look at these abilities more carefully in Section 4.3, which will help us to unpack this idea in more detail. But for now, the basic idea should be clear. Suppose Mary has never been to space but is reading an astronaut's autobiography which includes a rich description of the way it feels to walk on the moon. Reading this description Mary might think to herself 'so *that* [the feeling described in the book] is the way it feels to walk on the moon' and this thought could easily constitute knowledge (e.g., assuming that the description in the book is accurate). But Mary's new knowledge-that will not suffice for her to have reliable abilities to imagine and recognise the way it feels to walk on the moon, especially not when compared to someone who has had that experience. In which case, given the assumption that knowing-WIL ascription paradigmatically ascribe downstream knowledge, we will in many contexts intuit that Mary's new knowledge-that does not suffice for her to know what it is like to walk on the moon.

The explanation of (ii) relates to Lewis' claim that while experience is *not* the only *possible* teacher when it comes to gaining WIL-knowledge and the abilities he identified that knowledge with, it is the *best* teacher with respect to that knowledge and those abilities. That is, having an experience of Φ-ing is usually the best, and often the only practicable, way to gain abilities to imagine, recognise, and remember experiences of Φ-ing (these claims will be qualified somewhat in Section 5, but not in a way that conflicts with the key ideas here). In which case if knowing-WIL ascriptions are paradigmatically used to attribute a form of downstream knowledge that entails the possession of such abilities then it makes sense that, in most contexts, we will assume that having had such an experience is a requirement of someone's knowing what it is like to Φ.

The explanation of (iii) can start with the observation that if one thinks of WIL-knowledge as a form of downstream knowledge then some relevant phenomenal way of knowing condition will be an essential part of one's intellectualist analysis, given that mere upstream knowledge-that will not suffice for one to possess Lewis' abilities. Furthermore, the idea of downstream knowledge is motivated by a much larger set of considerations concerning not only the truth conditions of knowing-WIL ascriptions, but also knowing-wh ascriptions in general, and even some uses of knowing-that ascriptions. And it is also motivated by Hawley's related work on the client's interests in tracking reliable performers. From this perspective then the fact that mere knowing-that often appears to be insufficient for possessing different forms of knowing-wh, including but not limited to WIL-knowledge, can be given a unified explanation in terms of how we use knowledge ascriptions to identify reliable performers.

What about redundancy cases? If the downstream-use hypothesis is correct then we might expect there to also be redundancy cases for knowing-WIL, that is, cases where intuitively someone possesses WIL-knowledge despite their relevant true belief failing to meet some orthodox condition on knowing-that, like the anti-luck or justification condition. The possible existence of such cases is almost never discussed in the literature – the one exception I know being Currie (2020: 89) – but I do think there are such cases, and their existence provides further support for the downstream-use hypothesis.

Imagine Jackson's Mary again before she has left her room.[4] One day pre-release Mary is told, by a usually reliable source, that she will be given brief access to a previously locked cupboard within her room, which contains thousands of closed white envelopes each of which contains a red-coloured sheet of paper. Unbeknownst to Mary, this information is wrong and all but one of the envelopes has a green sheet of paper in it. Luckily, Mary happens to grab the one envelope with a red sheet of paper in it, and then the cupboard is locked again. Looking now at the red paper Mary comes to truly believe that *this* is the way it feels to see something red. Doesn't that true belief constitute a genuine state of knowledge for Mary, namely, knowledge of what it is like to see something red? At least when the client's perspective is salient (e.g., a context where someone is concerned with whether Mary could now fetch them the red

---

[4] This case is adapted from one in Cath (2023).

tube in an unlabelled box of paints), I suspect we will find the intuition that she does possess this knowledge, even though her true belief is 'gettierized' and hence she does not meet the standard anti-luck condition on knowledge.

Some support for this position comes from the fact that Currie (2020) reaches similar conclusions and gives his own example of a case where he thinks WIL-knowledge is present in a Gettier-style situation. Furthermore, I think support for this idea that WIL-knowledge is consistent with Gettier-style luck can also be found in Lewis' claim that experience is the best, but not the only possible, teacher when it comes to WIL-knowledge.

When Lewis made this claim what he had in mind were cases where someone gains abilities to imagine, recognise, and remember experiences of Φ-ing without ever having Φ-ed themselves. The specific scenarios that Lewis imagined were metaphysically possible cases where, by advanced neuroscience or magic (one could also appeal to cases involving incredible coincidences like swampman), a person is put into the same underlying types of physical states that someone comes to be in when they come to know what it is like smell a skunk on the basis of having smelled a skunk themselves. Lewis assumes that in such a scenario this person would know what it is like to smell a skunk, despite never having smelled a skunk themselves.

Lewis' position here makes sense when we think of his abilities, or at least his abilities to imagine and recognise, as these abilities are plausibly downstream states themselves. That is, any etiological properties of how a person came to acquire a putative ability to imagine or recognise what it is like to Φ are irrelevant to whether or not they actually possess that ability. All that is relevant is, looking downstream, whether they would successfully imagine what it is like to Φ-ing, or recognise an experience of Φ-ing, in certain relevant circumstances.

The case of the ability to remember experiences of Φ-ing is different though. Like any ability it is a downstream state in the sense that possessing it is roughly a matter of whether someone would successfully perform a certain kind of action in the right circumstances. However, for a mental action to be an action of *remembering* an experiencing of Φ-ing one must satisfy the upstream condition of having had such an experience at some point in the past. So, in the neuroscience and magic situations that Lewis imagines the subject would only have an ability to have *apparent* memories of smelling a skunk.[5] But given that Lewis

---

[5] One might object that even a newly materialised swampman has the *ability* to remember experiences they have not had yet. After all, while I have never travelled to India, surely, I have the ability to remember what it is like to travel in India, I have just never had the opportunity to exercise it. But this worry merely reveals the care we need to take in making ability ascriptions, given that they are always evaluated relative to contextually relevant sets of circumstances which are often left unstated. So, I have the ability to remember what it is like to travel in India *in circumstances where I have travelled in India*. For if I were to travel in India I could form and later

thinks that such a subject would still know what it is like to smell a skunk, it seems he was at least inclined not to take the ability to have genuine memories of the experience of Φ-ing to be a necessary condition for knowing what it is like to Φ. Also, later in his discussion Lewis (1988: 98) notes the possibility that over time one might lose one's ability to remember one's past experiences of eating vegemite whilst still retaining one's ability to imagine experiences of eating vegemite. And while Lewis does not explicitly state that in such a circumstance one would still know what it is like to taste vegemite, in context it reads (to me at least) that he is assuming that would be the case. Anyway, regardless of how we should interpret Lewis, I think the earlier considerations suggest that the ability to remember experiences of Φ-ing may not be a strictly necessary condition for knowing what it is like to Φ although usually we would expect someone who knows what it is like to Φ to have this ability (for this reason I will often talk of the memory condition as if it is on an equal footing to the imagination and recognition conditions).

4.3 Objectual Abilities

To further clarify and fill out this proposal that WIL-knowledge is a form of downstream knowledge, I want to say more now about how I think we should interpret these abilities to imagine, remember, and recognise. One simple point about how to interpret the ability to imagine condition is that it involves an ability to imagine the experience of Φ-ing itself – or, equivalently, imagine the way it feels to Φ itself – rather than just a mere ability to, say, imagine *that* the experience of Φ-ing is like such-and-such. So, if you eat Dutch liquorice for the first time afterwards it is true that you will be able to imagine *that* the experience of eating Dutch liquorice is comparable to experiences of eating other very salty things. But that is an ability you would've had before ever eating Dutch liquorice, and it is not the kind of ability at issue here. Rather, the relevant ability that you gain is an ability to imagine the way it feels to eat Dutch liquorice itself, you can in some sense make that taste experience present to one's mind again.

This clarification relates to the fact that Lewis (1988: fn.12) regards the ability to imagine, remember, and recognise an experience E as being just the same thing as an ability to imagine, remember, and recognise *what it is like* to have experience E. Note that when described in the latter way the same

---

recall memories of how it felt. But I do not have the ability to remember travelling in India *in my currently normal circumstances*. For those circumstances are ones in which I have never travelled to India, so I have no memories to recall of India and how it feels to travel there. And it is this kind of ability that matters to Lewis (as otherwise he would have to say that Mary has the ability to remember experiences of seeing something red before leaving her room).

ambiguity that we found in knowing-WIL ascriptions will arise for these ability conditions given the use of ambiguous 'what it is like' phrase. That is, if we take the ability to imagine what it is like to Φ condition, for example, and where w is the way it feels to Φ, we can interpret this ability as either: (i) an ability to imagine *that* w is the way it feels to Φ, or (ii) an ability to imagine w itself.[6] And the suggestion just made is that the objectual interpretation (ii) is the relevant one when interpreting the ability to imagine condition.

What is involved in making an experience of Φ-ing present to one's mind through one's imagining of that experience? Roughly following Paul (2015b: 476) – who suggests that when we have a new experience, we gain abilities to 'imagine, recognize, and cognitively model possible future experiences of this kind' – I take it that the relevant idea is one of cognitive modelling or simulating an experience in one's imagination. So, when one imagines, say, the experience of eating Dutch liquorice that mental event of imagining is an imagining of that target experience in part because it itself possesses some of the same phenomenal properties as that target experience.

The ability to remember the experience of eating Dutch liquorice will then be analysed in the same way but when one simulates that experience in one's imagination, that imagining must relate one in some appropriate way to one's own past experiences of eating Dutch liquorice. The recognition ability should also be interpreted as an ability to recognise an experience itself, rather than just recognise that p, for some proposition p concerning the way it feels to Φ. So, if one knows what it is like to have a panic attack, having had panic attacks before, then if one has that experience again one may well recognise the experience itself – that is, one will recognise the feeling involved in having a panic attack – rather than merely recognising *that*, say, the experience one is having is an experience of having a panic attack; as even if one had never had a panic attack before one might recognise that one is having a panic attack on the basis of one's prior knowledge of the typical causes and symptoms involved in a panic attack.

When it comes to possessing objectual WIL-knowledge it might suffice to possess these abilities to objectually imagine, remember, and recognise the relevant experience. But as interrogative WIL-knowledge is a form of propositional knowledge one will also need an ability or disposition to make relevant propositional judgements when one exercises these objectual abilities. So, possessing interrogative knowledge of what it is like eat Dutch liquorice is not only a matter of having an ability to bring that experience to mind, but being able to form an occurrent judgement that *this* is the way it feels to eat Dutch liquorice when one imagines, remembers, or recognises that experience.

---

[6] For discussion see D'Ambrosio and Stoljar (2021).

The full view here then is that interrogative WIL-knowledge is a form of downstream knowledge defined in terms of abilities to objectually imagine, remember, and recognise experiences, and an ability to make relevant propositional judgements when exercising those abilities. And the relevant forms of objectual imagining and remembering will be objectual and simulative in the way defined earlier, that is, the imagining shares some phenomenal properties with the target experience, and it is an imagining *of* that experience at least partly in virtue of simulating it.

There are two further qualifications we need to make about this notion of objectually and simulatively imagining an experience. One obvious qualification is that 'bringing an experience to mind' again in one's imagination is not the same thing as actually having that experience again. This point can be accommodated nicely within the framework of mental simulation because, in general, simulations almost always differ in significant ways from what they simulate. Think of, say, the differences in scale between a physical model of an America's Cup yacht used for testing in a wind tunnel versus the actual yacht it is a simulation of, or the deep ontological differences between the actual yacht and a computer simulation of it. Similarly, when it comes to simulating an experience in one's imagination, we should expect the relevant event of imagining to differ in notable ways from the target experience that it is a simulation of. And candidate differences might be that the imagining is typically less vivid and intense, and it may lack many of the phenomenal properties possessed by the target experience and/or possess other phenomenal properties (e.g., connected to the characteristic phenomenology of imagining) not possessed by the target experience, and so on. Nonetheless, as the simulative imagining will share some actual phenomenal properties with the relevant target experience – rather than, say, sharing mere structural properties – there is still a good sense in which we can say that one is bringing the experience to mind when one imagines it in this way. And a notable consequence of these points is that someone's ability to simulatively imagine an experience can be evaluated as more or less accurate, depending on how closely the phenomenal properties of the imaginings one has when one exercises that ability match those of the target experience itself (this idea will be important in Section 5.4).

The other qualification is that when an experience is sufficiently complex then one may only be able to imagine different parts of that complex experience at any one time. Consider the difference between simple sensory experiences – like, say, the experience of smelling basil, seeing something green, or hearing a D flat note played on a piano – versus experiences that have very complex structures involving lots of different events over time and different sensory modalities and emotional and cognitive phenomenology – like, say, the experience of exploring Tokyo as a tourist, or being a parent, or grieving the loss of a loved one.

The way it feels to have one of these simple experiences is, arguably, something that can be fully present to one's mind at one time, so when you have an experience of smelling basil the phenomenal properties which constitute that experience are fully present to one's mind. But this is not the case with the more complex experiences. For such experiences don't feel just one specific way, as these experiences are composed of lots of different sub-experiences which have different phenomenal properties, which are not instantiated together at any one time. So, when we talk about the way these complex experiences feel we will normally be talking about a range of different sub-experiences that can be involved in that complex experience, and their constituent phenomenal properties, or perhaps one of the sub-experiences which is especially salient when people think about the relevant type of experience – like, say, the distinctive feelings of love, concern, and responsibility, that are paradigmatically involved in the experience of being a parent (Paul 2015b: 485).

Now think about what is involved in objectually imagining or remembering one of the simple versus one of the complex experiences. When one simulatively imagines or remembers an experience of, say, tasting something lemony you don't literally have such an experience. But with simple experiences like that there is still a good sense in which you are imagining the full way it feels to have that experience, it is just that your mental act of imagining manages to have that full experience as its direct intentional object despite only being a partial simulation of it. However, when you imagine or remember a more complex experience, like say the experience of exploring Tokyo, you imagine that complex experience more indirectly in the sense that you succeed in imagining it by imagining different sub-experiences involved in that complex experience and partially simulating their respective phenomenal properties. So, if you have explored Tokyo and then you try to reimagine that experience you might first remember the way it feels to walk around the Shibuya scramble, and then you might move to reimagining the way it feels to wander down the quieter back streets, and so on. And as you do this your cognitive modelling of the complex experience will likely draw upon, and perhaps be partially constituted by, propositional imaginings and semantic memories, as well as simulative imaginings and memories.

4.4 Phenomenal Concepts and Downstream Intellectualism

Unlike other forms of qualified intellectualism, the view of downstream intellectualism developed earlier made no appeal to any notion of special concepts.

It is worth clarifying then that downstream intellectualism is consistent with the idea that WIL-knowledge involves the possession of phenomenal concepts. It is true that accounts of phenomenal concepts on which they are experience entailing do not fit naturally with downstream intellectualism given that entailing that one has had an experience of Φ-ing is kind of upstream condition (at least for standing states of WIL-knowledge possessed after the relevant experience has ended). But there are other accounts of phenomenal concepts which fit more naturally with downstream intellectualism because they characterise phenomenal concepts in terms of upstream recognitional abilities. And the view of the phenomenal concepts recently offered by Lee (2023) fits nicely with downstream intellectualism because it is a view on which a phenomenal concept of an experience is a mental representation of it that is: (i) defined in terms of its psychological role in enabling not only abilities to recognise such experiences and think about what they are like, but also to imagine these experiences, and (ii) possessing such a concept does not entail having had such an experience oneself.

A proponent of downstream intellectualism might appeal then to Lee's account of phenomenal concepts as part of an explanation of how states of WIL-knowledge can entail the possession of abilities to imagine and recognise, with the idea being that one has to not only know a proposition that answers the embedded WIL-question but in possessing that knowledge one has to possess a phenomenal concept. But a downstream intellectualist may also choose not to build an account of phenomenal concepts into their view, and there might be advantages to doing that.

Again, there are useful comparisons with issues in the knowing-how literature. As discussed in Section 3.2, one way of developing a qualified intellectualism for knowing-how is to appeal to some disposition-entailing notion of a practical mode of presentation. Those moves are quite closely analogous then to Lee's (2023) notion of phenomenal concepts as a special ability-enabling concept of the way it feels to have the relevant experience. But in the knowing-how literature not all qualified intellectualists appeal to practical modes of presentation. Rather, some appeal to practical ways of being in a propositional attitude state (Waights Hickman 2019; Cath 2020), rather than practical constituent concepts of the propositional content of that state, or practical ways of entertaining that content in thought. Cath (2020), for example, offers a view on which being in the relevant propositional attitude state is itself a matter of possessing certain practical dispositions, and one might offer a similar view in explaining how the true belief states involved in possessing WIL-knowledge entail abilities to imagine and recognise. Relatedly, these versions of qualified intellectualism for knowing-how and WIL-knowledge, which eschew practical/phenomenal concepts or modes of presentation, could be motivated by similar concerns including the desire to sidestep arguments that such special concepts or modes of presentation simply do not exist[7] or that these notions ultimately do not help to address the problems they are introduced to address.[8]

These choices are related to much larger choices between different accounts of the contents and nature of propositional attitude states, and their relation to the sets of dispositions or abilities they are most closely associated with. For example, we might think of these dispositions or abilities as something that is distinct from and explained by relevant representational and/or functional properties of the propositional attitude state. Or, alternatively, we think might of the propositional attitude state as something partly constituted by those dispositions or abilities, as on dispositional theories of the attitudes like Schwitzgebel (2013). I will not wade into these deeper waters here, for it will suffice to note that downstream intellectualism could be developed in different ways depending on one's positions on these larger issues.

5 Testimony and Partial WIL-Knowledge

In *What It Is Like to Go to War* the Vietnam War veteran Karl Marlantes aims 'to explain what it was like for me to go to war' (2011: 255). And Marlantes makes it clear in his introduction that part of the audience that he wants to share his WIL-knowledge with includes people who have never been to war themselves, especially young people considering whether to enlist, and politicians deciding whether to send young people to war. From the perspective of the answer condition alone, Marlantes' aspirations make perfect sense. For Marlantes knows what it is like to go to war, which means that he knows true propositions that answer the question 'what is it like to go war' and he wants to share those answers with other people through his words. And Marlantes' ambition to communicate his WIL-knowledge is no aberration, as a bit of googling (try searching for 'what is it like' or 'how does it feel') quickly reveals lots of apparent attempts to do the same in books, YouTube videos, blogs, articles, and so on.

More generally, knowing-that and knowing-wh (Poston 2016) can often be shared via testimony, at least in suitably favourable circumstances (e.g., where the hearer has good reasons to trust the speaker, and is not aware of any defeaters for those reasons). So, if Sarah knows that the play starts at 8pm, and Sarah tells Sam this then, if she didn't already know this fact, Sam can easily come to know *that* the play starts at 8pm on the basis of Sarah's testimony. And based on this same testimony Sam can also come to know

---

[7] See, e.g., Ball (2009).   [8] See, e.g., Glick (2015).

when the play starts, given the plausible assumption that knowing when the play starts is just a matter of knowing a relevant propositional answer to the question 'when does the play start?' Similarly, if Sarah knows who is playing the lead role in the play, and she tells Sam this, then Sam can come to also know *who* is playing the lead role on the basis of Sarah's testimony, and so on. In which case, if we follow the answer condition and think of WIL-knowledge as a form of knowing-wh that can be analysed in terms of knowing-that – like knowing where, when, who, and so on. – then it seems we should expect that WIL-knowledge can also be shared via testimony. And similar points can be made for other forms of acquiring knowledge of propositions that answer a WIL-question without having the relevant experience oneself, including consulting sources like films or novels, or theories about the subjective character of such experiences, and so on.

But from the perspective of the experience condition, Marlantes' aspirations seem futile. For if WIL-knowledge requires experience then it cannot be transmitted or acquired from mere testimony. And the strong intuitions that support the experience condition often find expression in claims that WIL-knowledge cannot be communicated or gained through testimony or other sources that do not involve having the relevant experience. So, Paul (2014: 13) expresses this outlook when she writes that what we learn from the case of Mary is that 'stories, testimony, and theories aren't enough to teach you what it is like to have truly new types of experiences – you learn what it is like by actually having an experience of that type'.

The tension between the experience and answer conditions then seems to be reflected in a tension in our attitudes and practices concerning the relationship between WIL-knowledge and testimony. Now in Section 4, I argued that we can reconcile the apparent tension between the experience and answer conditions by viewing WIL-knowledge as a form of downstream knowledge. And one can appeal to that same framework again here to explain why WIL-knowledge cannot be easily acquired through testimony in a way that is consistent with the answer condition. The idea will be that WIL-knowledge cannot be easily acquired from mere testimony because it is a form of downstream knowledge that involves the possession of Lewis' abilities, and obviously such abilities cannot be easily acquired through mere testimony. If you tell me what it is like to eat durian, I might acquire some knowledge of truths about the way it feels to eat durian, but I will not thereby acquire an ability to imagine the experience of eating durian. And, more generally, any view on which WIL-knowledge is not only a matter of knowing the right kind of proposition, but knowing it in a phenomenal way, can likely appeal to that phenomenal way of knowing condition to explain why WIL-knowledge cannot be shared through testimony.

But now our apparent practices of trying to share and acquire WIL-knowledge through testimony present a challenge to such views, for if WIL-knowledge is partly a matter of possessing abilities that cannot be acquired through testimony, why do we sometimes act as if such knowledge can be acquired through testimony? I think this challenge reveals that the framework offered in Section 4 requires further qualifications and supplementations if it is to accommodate the full range of our attitudes and practices concerning how we think about and ascribe WIL-knowledge. In particular, what we need to bring in and develop is the idea that WIL-knowledge can come in different degrees and grades – that there can be *partial* WIL-knowledge – and then we need to examine how this idea can help us to resolve these tensions in our attitudes and practices concerning the possibility of acquiring WIL-knowledge through testimony and other means that do not require one to have had the experience in question.

5.1 Degrees of Knowing-Wh

It is easy to think of WIL-knowledge as a binary, all or nothing, matter. Either you have had the experience, in which case you will know what it is like, or you haven't, in which case you won't. Obviously, this outlook relates to the intu-itions that support the experience condition, and even if one agrees with Lewis that it is metaphysically possible to know what it is like to Φ without having had an experience of Φ-ing, one might still think there is always a sharp divide between those who have such knowledge, and those who do not.

But our discussion already contains materials which suggest that this binary view is too simplistic, and that we should expect there to be good sense in which we can distinguish different degrees and grades of WIL-knowledge. So, for example, one way of motivating the degree view for WIL-knowledge is by noting that Lewis' abilities look like abilities that one can possess to different degrees. In which case, if possessing WIL-knowledge is partly a matter of possessing such abilities one might expect that WIL-knowledge will in turn come in degrees. We'll look at this idea more carefully in Section 5.4.

A different, but complimentary, way to motivate the degreed view is to appeal to the answer condition and the fact that other forms of knowing-wh typically come in different degrees. This point relates to the linguistic fact that knowing-wh ascriptions are usually *gradeable* (Pavese 2017). This means such ascriptions can be modified by degree and adverbial modifiers like 'largely', 'in part', 'well', 'very well', and 'better than'. So, for example, we might say 'Marama knows in part why the Roman Empire fell' if Marama knows some, but not all, of the reasons why the Roman Empire fell. Or we might say 'Marama knows how the

Roman Empire collapsed better than Ari' if Marama knows more facts than Ari does about the way in which the Roman Empire collapsed. And as Pavese (2017) demonstrates in detail we can explain how knowing-wh comes in degrees in a way that is consistent with the assumption that knowing-wh can be analysed in terms of knowing-that, even if we assume (as is common) that knowing-that itself does not come in degrees. For the idea is not that knowing that p comes in different degrees, but that knowing-wh comes in different degrees because there can be more than one propositional answer to an embedded wh-question, so we can comparatively evaluate the different answers one might know to such a question with respect to how informative these answers are.

Given that knowing-WIL ascriptions are ascriptions of knowing-wh we should expect then to find that similar gradable constructions can be made for knowing-WIL. And that is the case. So, I might say 'Stephanie knows what it is like to live in Australia better than I do' because, while both of us live in Australia, she has lived here all her life, and has seen much more of the country than I have, while I only moved to Australia as an adult. Or we might say 'Unlike Ari, Marama only knows in part what it is like to live with cancer' if, say, Ari has been living through cancer treatments for a long time, whereas Marama has just received her diagnosis. These considerations suggest then that we should expect WIL-knowledge to come in different degrees (e.g., being more/less complete or precise) and grades (e.g., being evaluated as better/worse than someone's else's WIL-knowledge).

5.2 Gold, Silver, and Bronze WIL-knowledge

In earlier work (Cath 2019) I unpacked one way that WIL-knowledge can come in different degrees by drawing a tripartite distinction between what I called gold, silver, and bronze knowledge of propositions of the form 'w is a way it feels to Φ'. Applied to the example of going to war, I characterised these three forms of knowledge like so:

> *Gold WIL-Knowledge*. There is some way such that Mary knows that this way is a way that it feels to go to war, and Mary knows this proposition in a phenomenal way, in the sense that her concept of that way originated in acts of directly attending to the phenomenal properties of her own experiences of going to war.
> *Silver WIL-Knowledge*. There is some way such that Mary knows that this way is a way that it feels to go to war, and Mary knows this proposition in a phenomenal way, in the sense that her concept of that way originated in acts of directly attending to the phenomenal properties of her own experiences distinct from, but relevantly similar to, the experience of going to war (which she has not had).

> **Bronze WIL-knowledge**. There is some way such that Mary knows that this
> way is a way that it feels to go to war, and Mary knows this proposition in
> some non-phenomenal way.

Gold WIL-knowledge is the kind of knowledge of experience connected to the
intuitions which support the experience condition. Adapting ideas from Tye
(2011), I suggested that to possess gold WIL-knowledge one must have
a concept of the way it feels to Φ which originated in acts of attending to
one's own experiences of Φ-ing. So, Mary has gold WIL-knowledge just in case
she not only knows a relevant proposition of the form 'w is a way it feels to go to
war' but her knowledge involves a concept of the way it feels to go to war which
was formed in response to her own experiences of going to war. This is a kind of
'upstream' way of developing a phenomenal mode of knowing condition which
will entail the experience condition. In Section 5.4, I will consider how to think
of this gold, silver, bronze, framework in a way that it more clearly fits with the
downstream version of intellectualism I offered in Section 4. But before doing
that, it will be useful to just set up the gold, silver, bronze distinctions on their
own terms, and then show (Section 5.3) how they can help to solve the puzzles
around testimony.

At the other end of the spectrum from gold WIL-knowledge is bronze WIL-
knowledge. Consider someone who has never been to war but who wants to
learn something about what it is like to have that experience. What can do they
do? Well, they might read Marlantes' book, and then they could go further and
consult literature, art, or movies, or they might read the books of Nancy
Sherman (e.g., Sherman 2010), a philosopher who has not been to war herself,
but who is a prominent expert on the subjective experiences involved in going to
war and returning to civilian life, and has interviewed hundreds of veterans
about their experiences. Merely gaining this second-hand knowledge will
typically not put one in a position to satisfy the kind of phenomenal ways of
knowing conditions that qualified intellectualists add to their theories to accommodate the intuitions that support the experience condition. But consulting
sources like testimony, stories, and theories can provide one with knowledge
of propositions of the form 'w is a way it feels to go to war' that answer the
embedded WIL-question, 'what is it like to go to war?' And, in that sense, it can
be considered a form of WIL-knowledge.

Importantly, however, even if one has not been to war there are still ways in
which one's knowledge of truths of the form 'w is a way it feels to go to war'
could satisfy a kind of phenomenal way of knowing condition. These are
the cases I called silver WIL-knowledge. So, in contrast to mere bronze
WIL-knowledge, one might not only consult the books of Marlantes and

Sherman, or Remarque's famous novel *All Quiet on the Western Front*, but one might also have had relevantly similar experiences that one could now relate to the target experience of going to war based on what one has learned from such sources. If Mary had been an ambulance officer, for example, she might have had relevantly similar experiences of dealing with people in a state of shock, seeing traumatic injuries and witnessing their effects on people and feeling one's own emotional reactions to those situations, and so on. When reading about what it is like to go to war, Mary might note certain similarities between her own experiences and certain experiences involved in going to war, and that could help her to not only know, of some way *w*, that *w* is a way it feels to go to war, but she could also possess that knowledge in a phenomenal way. For Mary could possess that knowledge in a way which draws upon her abilities to simulatively imagine and remember the way it feels to have these relevantly similar experiences.

So, Mary, might use her own experiences as 'samples' – in the sense discussed by Walton (2015) – judging the way it feels to go to war must feel, in part, like *this*, where the demonstrative either picks out certain phenomenal properties of her relevantly similar experiences as an ambulance officer as she is having those experiences (this is the kind of case Walton discusses) or, more likely, her experiences of simulatively imagining or remembering such experiences (Cath 2019, 2022). Or the demonstrative might just pick out features of Mary's attempt to imagine the target experience of going to war directly (rather than imagining the similar experiences and then judging that they are like the target experience), but where that attempt draws on her abilities to imagine and remember these distinct but relevantly similar experiences. Kind (2020) introduces the useful concept of *imaginative scaffolding* for this kind of process whereby one imagines a target experience one has not had by way of making additions, subtractions, and modifications to one's imaginings of experiences that one has had. So, Mary might try to imagine the way it feels to be in a combat situation directly but achieve a more accurate and informative imagining of that experience than someone who had never had any relevantly similar experiences. The role of sources like testimony, stories, and theories, in supporting this kind of silver WIL-knowledge is that it can serve as a guide to one's attempts at imagining the target experience, and at drawing the right connections between one's past experiences and the target experience.

Importantly, there may be principled limits to what kinds of experiences we can gain silver WIL-knowledge of. As Kind (2020) and Werner (2023) discuss it might be that some experiences, like simple sensory experiences, are 'undifferentiated wholes' (Kind 2020: 153) or 'atomic experiences' (Werner 2023: 177) which lack any phenomenal structure or complexity. And if that is the case then there may be no relevant shared properties between this simple experience and other experiences, which someone who had only had the later experiences could use as a basis for imagining the simple experience. As Kind notes, whether there are any atomic experiences like this is not clear, and prima facie candidates may turn out to have more complex structures on closer inspection. But if there are atomic experiences this might help to explain why, barring the kinds of remote possibilities that Lewis discussed (involving magic or future neuroscience), it seems to be a plausible hypothesis about human psychology that some kinds of very simple experiences (like seeing something red) can't be simulatively imagined without having had an experience of that kind oneself. In which case, it may be that a restricted version of the experience condition is true where it is restricted both to normal circumstances, to rule out the remote possibilities that Lewis discussed, and to atomic experiences, to rule out cases where one succeeds in obtaining partial WIL-knowledge via one's distinct but relevantly similar experiences.

Returning to bronze WIL-knowledge, it is worth clarifying that in saying that bronze WIL-knowledge is non-phenomenal the idea is not that any associated occurrent judgements would lack any phenomenal properties, rather the idea is just that one's knowledge does not draw upon one's acquaintance with the phenomenal properties of one's own experiences in either of the respective ways described for gold and silver WIL-knowledge. So, the notion of bronze WIL-knowledge is consistent with possible views on which all knowledge might be said to be phenomenal in a certain sense, like, say, a view on which knowing that p will always involve a disposition to form a conscious judgement that p which has some kind of cognitive phenomenology.

It is also worth noting that bronze WIL-knowledge itself can come in degrees (Cath 2019: 11). So, consider two people each of whom has been studying the subjective experiences involved in going to war, but neither of whom has been to war themselves and neither of them have had any relevantly similar experiences which that they can draw on in conceptualising the experiences involved in going to war. But one of these people has simply read and studied more than the other, such that the first person has studied only the negatively valenced feelings involved in going to war, whereas the second has studied those and the positively valenced feelings (like feelings of elation that people can have during combat experiences). In this situation it would make sense to say that the second person knows more about what it is like to go to war than the first. The difference between these two subjects is a difference in the *quantity* of information that they possess, that is, it is a difference in the number of answers they know to the WIL-question, or the completeness of the answers that they know. On the other hand, the differences between gold, silver, and bronze WIL-knowledge also concern the *quality* of those answers or one's epistemic access to those answers. And, as Pavese (2017) discusses, knowing-wh ascriptions in general are gradable in both quantitative and qualitative senses so this, again, fits with more general patterns of how we ascribe knowing-wh.

5.3 Solving the Testimony Puzzles

The solution to the puzzles around testimony is implicit in the ideas just discussed but its exact form needs to be spelled out carefully. The solution, as I will develop it here, appeals to just two key ideas. The first idea is that in stereotypical contexts, a 'S knows what it is like Φ' ascription (on its interrogative interpretation) will be judged to be true just in case the subject knows a relevant proposition, *and* they also possess this knowledge in a phenomenal way. This idea is then used to explain the force, and partial correctness, of our intuitions about the inability to acquire WIL-knowledge from testimony; with that explanation differing in some of its details depending on whether we ultimately analyse the phenomenal way of knowing condition in terms of a requirement that either directly entails that we have had certain experiences, or that entails that we have certain abilities, as I advocated in Section 4.

If we go with the former idea, then we will explain the intuitions about WIL-knowledge not being transmittable via testimony in terms of the stereotypical use claim and the inability of testimony to transmit experiences. For on this approach the phenomenal way of knowing condition entails that one has gold WIL-knowledge which, of course, requires one to have had an experience of Φ-ing. On the other hand, if we go with the latter idea – which I take to be the better one given the considerations discussed in Section 4 and also subsequently in this section – then we will explain the intuitions about WIL-knowledge not being transmittable via testimony in terms of the stereotypical use claim and the difficulty of acquiring abilities through mere testimony. For downstream knowledge requires one to have abilities to simulatively imagine and recognise experiences of Φ-ing. But, as discussed before, this will often still mean that the subject has had an experience of Φ-ing themselves – and thereby has gold WIL-knowledge on that basis – because, following Lewis (1988: 77), the 'best teacher' of those abilities is having the experience oneself.

But while having an experience is the best teacher for gaining such abilities it is not the only possible teacher, and those other possible teachers are not limited to just the kinds of remote possibilities that Lewis discussed (being put into the relevant physical states through magic or future neuroscience). For, and this is the second key idea, at least with respect to complex/non-atomic experiences, people can develop abilities to imagine and cognitively model experiences they have not had themselves, by drawing on their imaginative abilities gained from having distinct but relevantly similar experiences. And these imaginings of experiences they have not had can then be incorporated into their knowledge of what that target experience is like, giving one silver WIL-knowledge. And while testimony cannot transmit silver WIL-knowledge – because it also involves abilities that cannot be transmitted by mere testimony – it can transmit bronze WIL-knowledge and that knowledge can play a role in our acquiring silver-WIL knowledge by informing us of these similarities and providing information that can guide our attempts to better imagine experiences we have not had ourselves.

The reason then that there is an apparent tension in our practices and attitudes towards the possibility of sharing WIL-knowledge with those who have not had the relevant experiences, is that, on the one hand, when we make unqualified utterances of the form 'S knows what it is like to Φ' we will usually communicate that someone has had an experience of Φ-ing (either because the phenomenal way of knowing condition entails that they have had such an experience or because it entails that they have certain abilities which usually indicate that someone has had such an experience). But, on the other hand, many of our practices around WIL-knowledge suggest that we are committed, at least implicitly, to the possibility of people acquiring WIL-knowledge with respect to experiences they have not had themselves.

The idea that WIL-knowledge can come in different degrees and grades allows us to acknowledge that there can be an epistemic payoff from people's attempts to share and acquire WIL-knowledge, whilst still acknowledging that there are forms of WIL-knowledge that are very difficult, and in some cases practically impossible, for one to acquire without one having had the relevant target experience oneself.

5.4 Degrees of Abilities

The gold, silver, and bronze distinctions are a useful way of thinking about how WIL-knowledge can come in different degrees and grades, as evidenced by how these distinctions can be used to illuminate the puzzles around testimony, and how these distinctions have also been fruitfully applied to other issues.[9] But, with respect to partial WIL-knowledge, I do not think these distinctions are exhaustive, and there are other ways to think of how WIL-knowledge can come in different degrees that might capture more detailed aspects of this phenomenon.

They are not exhaustive because, for example, we may want to distinguish a further grade of WIL-knowledge, what we could call *platinum* knowledge of experience. This would be the knowledge one has when, for some way *w*, one

---

[9] See, e.g., Allen (2022), Fürst (2023), and Cawston and Wildman (2023).

knows that w is a way it feels to Φ as one is having an experience of Φ-ing. This may seem to a better grade of WIL-knowledge than gold, given the fact that reimagining an experience is not the same thing as reliving it. So, think of eating vegemite for the first time, and knowing as one has that experience, that *this* is the way it feels to vegemite. One might think that the knowledge one has at that moment of what it is like to eat vegemite is better than the knowledge one will have of it later, after the experience has ended, because as one is having that experience the phenomenal properties that constitute it will be more vividly and precisely present to one's mind than they will be later on when one merely recalls the experience in one's imagination.

People who have had the same experiences can also differ later in the quality of their respective abilities to imagine, remember, and recognise experiences of that type. So, suppose Marama and Jane have both eaten vegemite, in which case, they should both have gold knowledge of what it is like to eat vegemite, according to the definition in Cath (2019). But there could still be lots of different ways in which one of these two people might be said to know what it is like to eat vegemite better than the other. Perhaps Jane has only eaten vegemite a couple of times, and some years ago, and so while she can bring that experience back to mind in her imagination, when she does so her imaginings of it are not very vivid or precise. Marama, on the other hand, eats vegemite regularly which contributes to her having very good abilities to imagine and remember what it is like to eat vegemite. And Marama might also have better recognition abilities, so she might be able to recognise the difference between the experiences of eating vegemite versus eating marmite (which has a similar taste), whereas Jane might only be able to recognise the experience of eating vegemite in less demanding contexts (like when asked to distinguish it from an experience of eating jam).

There could also be cases where someone with silver WIL-knowledge will be in a better position to imagine the given target experience that they have not had themselves than someone who has had the experience and so has gold WIL-knowledge. Take the ability to imagine what it is like to look around a certain room and consider two people, one of whom has looked around that room many times, and the other who has never been in that room but has seen a photo of it. Normally, it would be natural and justifiable to assume that the first person will have better abilities to imagine the experience of looking around the room, but this need not always be the case. For example, if the first person has severe aphantasia, but the second person has very good abilities to perform visual imagination tasks, then the second person may have better abilities to imagine this experience.

One lesson suggested by these examples is that people can possess Lewis' abilities to different degrees. And, relatedly, while having an experience is often the only practical way of gaining abilities to imagine and recognise experiences of that type, there is no determinate path from having had an experience to possessing those abilities to any given degree. Another lesson is that, given the connections between WIL-knowledge and Lewis' abilities, we should expect that there will also be close connections between how WIL-knowledge can come in different grades and degrees and how these abilities can come in different degrees. Lee (2023) develops a rich view of this broad kind in relation to his account of phenomenal concepts mentioned in Section 4.4, and this idea also follows naturally from our earlier discussion of downstream intellectualism and how the ability to imagine condition should be interpreted in terms of simulatively imagining the target experience. For the extent to which an event of imagining shares phenomenal properties with the target experience will clearly be a matter of degree.

To help illustrate some of these points, consider what a perfect imaginative simulation of an experience would be. Like Nozick's 'experience machine', with respect to its constituent phenomenal properties it would be subjectively indistinguishable from the target experience it simulates, with the only difference being its non-standard cause. So, if you intended, say, to reimagine what it is like for you to sit in your favourite park on a summer's day you would have an experience which would be indistinguishable from, and have the exact same phenomenal properties as, a normal experience of you sitting in that park on a summer's day; it is just that the *cause* of your experience would be your intention to imagine an experience of that type rather than an event of sitting in the park.

Of course, for us normal human beings, imagining an experience is not reliving it. But now think of one these hypothetical perfect imaginings and how it could be made to be more like a normal imperfect imagining by selectively removing, distorting, or adding phenomenal properties to it. That is a process that would clearly come in degrees, as one might just change the phenomenal greenness of the grass to a lurid lime green, or one might do that and remove the feeling or the sun on one's skin, or one might make both those changes and then also intensify the prickly feeling of the grass beneath one's body, and so on. This indicates how real people's partial and imperfect imaginings of the experience of Φ-ing might be compared to each other and considered better or worse, or more or less precise, and so on.

Furthermore, as Lee (2023: 191) shows the recognition ability can also come in different degrees. Lee gives the example of Ms. Scarlet who, like Jackson's Mary, is kept in a black and white room but on day *n* she is allowed to enter another room for 5 minutes. In that room are 100 colour chips, each of which is a different shade of red and is labelled with a term for the kind of visual experience Ms. Scarlet will have when looking at it, where one of these colour chips will induce scarlet experiences in Ms Scarlet and is labelled as such. At the end of day n, after looking at all the colour chips, Ms Scarlet is given a test where she has to identify the colour experiences induced by the colour chips again, but now the chips are not labelled. On day n, after she has looked at the colour chips for just 5 minutes, Ms. Scarlet will do very poorly on the test. But on each day after n Ms. Scarlet is allowed to see the same labelled colour chips again for five minutes each time, and afterwards she is given the same test. As the days go by, we would expect Ms. Scarlet to do better and better on the tests, as her abilities to recognise scarlet gradually improve with time and training.

So, the abilities to imagine and recognise experiences can come in different degrees of accuracy, depending on how many phenomenal properties are shared between one's imaginings of that experience and the target experience which they are imaginings of, or how well one can recognise experiences of that type. Furthermore, there are clearly close connections between, on the one hand, our assessments of WIL-knowledge as coming in different grades and degrees and, on the other hand, the degrees to which one possesses these abilities to imagine and recognise. For example, it is very plausible that Ms. Scarlet on day 100 knows what it is like to see something red *better* than she did on day 5, and that on day 5 she only knows *approximately* what it is like to see something scarlet, whereas she might know *exactly* what it is like on day 100.

In line with points made at the end of Section 4.4, how we ultimately explain these correspondences will differ depending on larger issues concerning the content and nature of propositional attitudes, and their relationship with the abilities they are closely associated with. So, for example, one might hold a 'Fregean' view according to which each day Ms Scarlet comes to stand in the knowledge relation to a new fine-grained proposition which provides a more complete answer to the question 'what is it like to see something scarlet?', and this is what explains the increasing accuracy of her abilities (cf. Pavese 2015 on practical senses and degrees of knowing-how). Or we might follow Lee's (2023) view on which Ms Scarlet's improving abilities are explained by her gaining new phenomenal concepts of scarlet experiences (i.e., a new mental representation which constitutes part of her belief state, rather than a new Fregean sense which is part of the believed proposition) each of which eliminates more 'phenomenal possibilities' (Lee 2023: 198) than the previous concepts. Or, if one held a dispositional view of the propositional attitudes (e.g., Schwitzgebel 2013), one might maintain that it is the differences in the accuracy of Ms. Scarlet's WIL-knowledge from one day to the next that are explained by, and grounded in, the changes in her different abilities from one day to the next, and not the other way around. I will not try to adjudicate here between these kinds of options. But on any of these views we can acknowledge that our judgements about WIL-knowledge coming in different degrees or grades will be intimately linked with our judgements about the degree to which one possesses these abilities to imagine and recognise experiences.

Relatedly, it is also likely that the degree to which a subject needs to possess abilities to imagine and recognise experiences of Φ-ing in order for the corresponding ascription of WIL-knowledge to be judged to be true will be a context sensitive matter. Recall the claim that, in stereotypical contexts, for a knowing-WIL ascription to be judged to be true the subject will need to know the right kind of proposition and in a phenomenal way, which will involve the possession of abilities to imagine and recognise the relevant experiences. The suggestion now then is that the degree to which one needs to be able to possess those abilities to count as knowing that proposition in a phenomenal way is itself a matter that is likely to be context sensitive. So, for example, when assessing an assertion that someone knows what it is like to drink a good pinot noir, the recognitional abilities required for the assertion to be judged to be true might be less exacting when the context of evaluation is a conversation amongst friends who get together to taste different wines than when it is a conversation amongst sommeliers.

This general approach, on which we think of degrees of WIL-knowledge in terms of these degreed abilities, fits more seamlessly with the view of downstream intellectualism I advocated for in Section 4 because, unlike the concepts of gold and silver WIL-knowledge, there is no upstream or 'backwards' looking experience condition (either for the same experience in the case of gold WIL-knowledge or similar experiences for silver WIL-knowledge), built directly into the account of degrees of WIL-knowledge itself. Rather we analyse WIL-knowledge, and how it can come in degrees, in terms of a form of downstream knowledge that entails the possession of certain abilities, and that knowledge can come in different degrees which either explains, or is explained by, those abilities coming in different degrees.

That said, usually one can reasonably assume that someone who has had an experience of Φ-ing will have better abilities to imagine experiences of that kind than someone who hasn't, and that someone who has had experiences which are importantly similar but distinct from the target experience of Φ-ing will have better abilities to imagine such experiences than someone who has had neither the target experience nor any relevantly similar experiences. Furthermore, it does seem plausible that, apart from the remote metaphysical possibilities that Lewis considers, there are certain very simple experiences which one wouldn't be able to simulatively imagine and recognise unless one has had an experience of that type in the past. In which case, as discussed earlier, there will be, in principle, limits on what kinds of silver WIL-knowledge we can achieve, and there will be a true version of the experience condition restricted to atomic experiences and normal circumstances. Together these points indicate why the gold, silver, bronze distinctions are a useful heuristic for thinking about how WIL-knowledge can come in different degrees, even if there are other more detailed and accurate ways of thinking of how WIL-knowledge can come in degrees. For in general one can safely assume that the gold, silver, and bronze distinctions will roughly correspond with greater to lesser degrees of the abilities to imagine, remember, and recognise experiences.

6 Pitfalls and Possibilities

Our experiences shape our identities, both individual and collective. Given the deep connections between experience and identity, and between experience and WIL-knowledge, any suggestion that people can have WIL-knowledge of experiences they have not had themselves can quickly set off serious alarm bells, including both epistemological concerns about whether we can achieve such knowledge, and related ethical concerns that there is something morally wrong with attempting to gain such knowledge. A common response to such concerns is to appeal (implicitly or explicitly) to the experience condition and deny the possibility of people achieving any WIL-knowledge of experiences they have not had themselves. But what I want to briefly explore now, in this closing section, is how we might navigate these concerns in such a way that we can acknowledge the important insights they raise, whilst still acknowledging the, in principle, possibility of people achieving partial WIL-knowledge of experiences they have not had.

6.1 Epistemic Arrogance and the Experience Condition

As Kind (2021) discusses, one common concern with the idea of people trying to obtain WIL-knowledge of the experiences of other people is that there is something arrogant about thinking that one could gain such knowledge by merely doing things like consulting testimony or reading a novel. There are also other related concerns, including that such attempts can constitute a form of epistemic trespassing, appropriation, or 'experience tourism', and that, as such, these attempts can serve to trivialise the experiences they supposedly aim to illuminate and, in some cases, even reinforce oppressive social structures they were meant to combat; concerns like this have been raised by various authors including Ngo (2017a) and Ramirez (2018, 2021) who raise them in relation to attempts to gain WIL-knowledge through the use of supposed simulations of the given target experience.

There are strong connections, I think, between these kinds of concerns and the intuitive appeal of the experience condition. For note that if this condition were true, without any qualifications, then trying to obtain WIL-knowledge of experiences that one has not had oneself – through activities of using one's imagination, together with, say, consulting literature, testimony, simulations, or theories about the relevant class of experiences – would be tantamount to trying to have the relevant experience oneself through engaging in such activities. And if having such an experience is part of what makes one a member of a given social group, then thinking that one can obtain WIL-knowledge through such activities would almost be tantamount to thinking that such activities could suffice to make one a member of that group.

But obviously it would be not only be arrogant and insensitive but absurd to think that engaging in such activities could give you the relevant experiences or make you a member of the relevant social group. If you have not been to war, no amount of reading Marlantes and Sherman's books will give you the experience of going to war, or make you a veteran. And if you are a white person, no amount of reading literature or phenomenological analyses of the experiences of living with racism (e.g., Ngo's own 2017b), or engaging with a supposed simulation of it like the virtual reality simulation *1,000 Cut Journey* (for discussion see Ramirez 2021) will give you the experience of living with racism, or make you a person of colour.

The accounts of downstream intellectualism and degrees of WIL-knowledge developed in Sections 4–5 allow us to agree that it would be absurd and arrogant to think that one could gain an experience-entailing form of WIL-knowledge from merely engaging with sources like testimony and simulations, and using one's imagination, and so on, whilst still acknowledging that one could possibly gain limited forms of partial WIL-knowledge from such actions.[10] For having partial WIL-knowledge – in the form of silver or even just bronze WIL-knowledge – with respect to a target experience of Φ-ing does not entail one's having had an experience of Φ-ing oneself.

However, as discussed earlier, in stereotypical contexts, an unqualified 'S knows what it is like to Φ' ascription will communicate that one has an

---

[10] Kind (2021: 249) appeals to the notion of *understanding* experiential perspectives other than one's own, on the grounds that understanding, unlike knowledge, comes in degrees. But this move isn't necessary given that, as discussed in Section 5.1, most forms of knowing-wh come in degrees even if knowing-that does not. And, by itself, just appealing to the notion of understanding won't suffice to address the issues here because the same intuitions that support the experience condition also arise for understanding what it is like to have experiences (e.g., intuitively, Mary not only doesn't know, but also doesn't understand, what it is like to see something red). In which case, one would still need to appeal here to something like the framework developed in Section 5.

experience of Φ-ing in virtue of having an experience or ability entailing form of WIL-knowledge. And this point helps to explain why people so readily hear claims about someone acquiring WIL-knowledge as communicating that they have had the corresponding experience, which in turns explain the deep resistance, and even animosity, that people can have to any suggestions that someone could gain WIL-knowledge about experiences they have not had themselves. For, so interpreted, the suggestion that someone can have WIL-knowledge of the experiences of other people from, say, imagination and testimony, or a VR simulation, is a suggestion that they can have the very same types of experiences themselves via such means, which is not only epistemically implausible but also arrogant and offensive.

But we can block these inferences from claims that someone knows what it is like to Φ to the conclusion that they must have had an experience of Φ-ing, by explicitly cancelling them, or by using qualified knowing-WIL ascriptions (adding modifiers like 'approximately', 'in part', or 'to some degree'), or by relying on features of the conversational context to do this work. So, for example, it would be perfectly reasonable for me to say: 'Neither of us have been to war, but Nancy Sherman knows what it is like better than I do.' For in making such an utterance I cancel any implication that either of us has been to war, and I communicate something true, namely, that Nancy Sherman knows a great deal many more truths about the way that the events involved in going to go to war can make a person feel. Relatedly, Lee (2023: 195) points out that for knowing-wh ascriptions in general an ascription of the form 'S knows approximately wh-Φ' does not entail an unqualified 'S knows wh-Φ' ascription, and so we should expect the same to be true for knowing-WIL ascriptions.

Importantly, the aforementioned points are consistent with endorsing concerns that attempts by people to acquire WIL-knowledge of experiences they have not had can sometimes be morally problematic, even if one grants that it is possible, in principle, for people to obtain partial WIL-knowledge through such attempts. And attempts to simulate the experiences of other people as a way of gaining WIL-knowledge often elicit such concerns. So, for example, in 2017 an Australian charity which runs a fundraising event called 'CEO sleepout' – where CEOs sleep outside for a night to raise money for the homeless – was widely criticised after footage came out from the event of CEOs wearing virtual reality headsets running a simulation of being homeless in an attempt 'to get a glimpse of the realities faced by the people who experience this everyday' (Zhou 2017).[11]

---

[11] Ramirez (2021: 99–100) discusses a similar case in the United States.

The images of wealthy CEOs trying to understand the experiences of homeless people by donning a VR headset were criticised on Twitter for being 'tone deaf' and even 'dystopian' (Zhou 2017). Some of the implied criticisms were epistemic in nature, with people rightly pointing to the vast differences between the experience a CEO would have in the virtual simulation (where they know the experience is not real, that it will soon be over, and that they can leave it at any time) and the real experiences of homelessness that the virtual experience is attempting to simulate. We'll return to these kinds of concerns in Section 6.3. But many of the criticisms, like the 'tone deaf' criticism, looked to be moral criticisms which could still be made even if one granted that people can, in principle, gain partial WIL-knowledge by using simulations like this. And there are lots of other moral criticisms that are often made about attempts to use VR as a supposed 'empathy machine'. For example, that one shouldn't need a VR simulation to know that we need to help the homeless or refugees, or that solitary confinement is cruel and should be abolished, and so we should just be focused on taking actions to address these problems, rather than trying to simulate these experiences. And there are related concerns that such simulations might serve to 'gamify' and trivialise the experiences they aim to simulate. Indeed, as Ngo (2017a) discusses, some attempts to simulate the experience of racism explicitly present themselves as games and their users as players.

There are plausibly many ways then in which attempts by one subject to gain WIL-knowledge of the experiences of other people can be morally problematic. But that important point doesn't reveal any, in principle, limitations to our epistemic capacities to gain partial WIL-knowledge about the experiences of other people. And, even focusing just on the moral issues, it would be a mistake to infer from these legitimate concerns about specific attempts to gain WIL-knowledge about other people, that *any* such attempt will always be morally problematic.

Indeed, it seems clear that sometimes people can have important moral obligations to attempt to gain partial WIL-knowledge of the experiences of other people. Consider, say, a non-disabled partner of a person living with a disability that significantly impacts many areas of their life. The non-disabled partner surely has an obligation to try and learn *something* about what it is like for their partner to live with that disability in an ableist society. The non-disabled partner may often fail in those attempts, and when they do succeed their WIL-knowledge will be partial and limited, but they should try to gain this knowledge despite those difficulties and limitations. The notion of partial WIL-knowledge allows us to make sense of how we can be subject to these kinds of obligations in a way that: (i) does not commit us to the arrogant idea that we could come to have the very same experiences and experiential knowledge as they do merely by talking with them, or engaging with literature or simulations, and so on, but (ii) still acknowledges that these are genuinely *epistemic* obligations to try to learn *something* about the experiential perspective of the other person as opposed to just being, say, mere obligations to listen with sympathy and concern when others talk about their experiences.

6.2 'No Comparison' Worries

However, is it really possible to achieve partial, but still non-trivial, WIL-knowledge of experiences we have not had? The idea of silver WIL-knowledge rested on the assumption that there can be similarities between one's own experiences and a relevant target experience that one has not had. But one might worry that often any such similarities will be so 'thin' that one will not be able to use them to meaningfully improve one's knowledge of the target experience. It might be that one can achieve some very limited kinds of bronze and even silver WIL-knowledge in such cases, but that knowledge will be uninformative and of little value.

This worry is most obvious when considering cases where the experience that a subject has not had is one that involves a sensory modality that this subject either does not have access to at all, or that they only have some very limited form of access to. Mary in her black-and-white room is an example of this kind. For when Mary is in her room, she only has access to black-and-white visual experiences which obviously form a poor basis for building imaginative models of coloured visual experiences. Similarly, Paul (2014: 106–7) discusses the case of a blind saxophonist who is given the opportunity to become sighted through surgery, and Paul claims that the saxophonist 'lacks the capacity to imaginatively represent the nature of this lived experience' (2014: 107). In these kinds of examples there is a strong case to be made that the 'distance' (Cath 2022: 9) or 'gulf' (Kind 2021: 237) between a subject's own experiences and the target experience which they have not had is too great for the former experiences to form any kind of basis for the subject to build an informative model in their imagination of that target experience.

There are good reasons then to think that in situations where one has only very limited access to a whole sensory modality, they will not be able to simulatively imagine experiences of that kind and have informative silver WIL-knowledge concerning them on that basis. But most of the cases where people try to acquire WIL-knowledge about other people's experiences, or possible experiences they could have themselves in the future, are not like this. Rather, they are cases involving complex experiences – like going to war, or living in a new country, or being a parent – with many experiential parts involving all kinds of sensory, affective, and cognitive phenomenal properties, some of which the person may have been acquainted with already in their own distinct but relevantly similar experiences. Is there any reason to think that the distance between experiences in cases like this will as problematically large as the distance between the experiences of two different sensory modalities?

6.3 Subjective Variations in Experience

One might think that when the background, and social location, of two subjects is very different then the distance between their experiences will be so significant that neither subject could ever have informative silver WIL-knowledge of the other's experiences. Paul (2014: 7–8), for example, expresses something like this assumption when she writes: 'If you are a man who has grown up and always lived in a rich Western country, you cannot know what it is like to be an impoverished woman living in Ethiopia, and if she has never left her village she cannot know what it is like to be you.'

One way to support this assumption, is to appeal to the further idea that differences in who we are can led to differences in how we experience the same type of event or action. Ramirez (2021), for example, appeals to this kind of idea in critiquing attempts to use VR simulations to understand the experiences of other people, and more specifically he appeals to his own 'intersectional theory' of experience according to 'which the content of an individual person's experience, at any given time, is going to be shaped not only by where they happen to be looking, but also by the effects that their internalized concepts of race, gender, class, nationality, etc., have on those experiences' (Ramirez 2021: 110). Appealing to this theory, Ramirez's idea is that there will usually be significant differences in the intersectional identities of the intended users of a VR simulation of the experience of Φ-ing, versus the intersectional identities of the group of people who are having the relevant target experiences of Φ-ing. In which case, if the intended users of the VR simulation were to actually have an experience of Φ-ing their resulting experiences would be very different from the experiences of the people having the target experiences of Φ-ing, and that means the VR simulation could at best help someone to know what it would be like for *themselves* to Φ not what it is like for that group of people to Φ. As Ramirez (2018) states this idea: 'For all its potential, VR can't show us what it's like to *be* someone else. To echo Nagel, it can only reveal what it would be like for *us* to have these experiences.'

Ramirez's conclusion here relates to Stoljar's claim, discussed in Section 3.1, that there are different ways of disambiguating the two subject positions – one for an agent of the event, and one for an experiencer of the event – in the logical form of an embedded WIL-question. Consider (1):

(1)   Marama knows what it is like to go caving.

The natural interpretation of (1) in many contexts would be one on which Marama is both the experiencer and the agent. On Stoljar's semantics this interpretation is represented like so:

(1.1)   Marama knows what it is like to *Marama* for *Marama* to go caving.

But there could be contexts where we are interested in whether Marama knows what it is like for Bill to go caving or, more precisely, what it is like for Bill to experience Bills' action of going caving. On Stoljar's semantics this interpretation is represented like so:

(1.2)   Marama knows what it is like to *Bill* for *Bill* to go caving.

Now, related to Ramirez's discussion, we can easily imagine circumstances in which (1.1) is true but (1.2) is false, due to differences between Marama and Bill. So, perhaps Marama has been caving and so she knows what her going caving is like for herself, but Marama does not suffer from claustrophobia whereas Bill does. In which case, the way that Bill feels when he goes caving will be significantly different, and consequently Marama may fail to know what it is like for Bill when he goes caving. For Marama may not be able to accurately imagine the way that it feels to go caving whilst suffering from claustrophobia, and she may not even be aware that Bill has claustrophobia which might lead her to falsely believe that the way it feels for Bill when he goes caving is very similar to the way it feels for herself when she goes caving.

The psychological difference between Marama and Bill which leads to their different experiences does not stem from differences in their intersectional identities. But the larger idea is the same as Ramirez's, namely, that differences in who we are – understood in a broad way to include our background experiences and knowledge, psychological dispositions, and social location, and so on – can led to differences in the way we experience the same event or action. So, for example, as Ngo (2017a: 113–15) discusses, a white person engaging with a simulation of being subjected to micro-level expressions of racism may come away with the mistaken impression that such acts are not actually racist or that the events of being subjected to those acts are not that bad, because if *they* were to encounter such events in their life those events would not make them the feel the same way as a person of colour. This is because a person of colour has knowledge and past experiences which allow them to interpret the racist significance of such acts more accurately, and that in turn could result in those acts making them feel a very different way from how a white person would feel if they were to somehow encounter those acts in real life, or representations of such acts in a simulation.

I think these broadly related insights from Ngo and Ramirez are sound and important, as they identify a source of significant errors – in the form of inaccurate imaginings of the target experience and false beliefs about the way it feels to have that experience – that can happen when people try to gain WIL-knowledge of the experiences of other people. But there is also a danger, I think, of overestimating the wider significance of this fact that the content and character of our experiences can be sensitive to differences in who we are.

So, for example, Ramirez concludes, by way of appealing to his intersectional thesis, that we should reject claims made by VR developers that their simulations 'can give you these kinds of experiences' (Ramirez 2021: 100) so that 'you experience what it is like for someone else to have these experiences, from their point of view' (Ramirez 2021: 108). This is a correct conclusion to draw, I think, for given the fact that the way our experiences feel can be influenced by differences in who we are, and other differences between simulation experiences and their targets, like differences in duration (Bloom 2017), it would be extremely naïve to hold that a VR simulation could actually give you an experience of the same type as the relevant target experience. But as well as this reasonable conclusion should we also infer the further, and much stronger, conclusion that such simulations could never help someone to gain any partial knowledge of what it is like for the relevant group of people to have the relevant target experience?

Ramirez seems to be committed to this kind of further conclusion because, for example, he claims that 'VR and AR simulations can't give us access to the inner lives of other people' (2021: 105) apart from very limited 'base cases' where there are no relevant psychological differences between the person using the VR simulation and the people having the relevant experience. Relatedly, Ramirez advocates thinking of VR simulations as only being able to enhance *sympathy* and not *empathy* (2021: 121). And this suggests that Ramirez thinks of VR simulations as having no epistemic value with respect to learning something about the experiences of other people, given that when sympathy is distinguished from empathy the idea is usually that the former is merely a matter of feeling concern for the other person rather than feeling what they feel (affective empathy) or knowing how they feel (cognitive empathy).

But this inference from the claim that VR simulations cannot give you the experiences of other people to the conclusion they cannot give you any know-ledge of what those experiences are like only makes sense if we accept the experience condition and think of all WIL-knowledge in an experience entailing and binary way. For once we have the idea of WIL-knowledge coming in degrees we can make sense of the, in principle, possibility of such simulations helping one to gain partial WIL-knowledge concerning what the relevant target experiences are like. For the fact that a simulation experience is not the same experience as the target experience it is aiming to simulate is consistent with it still sharing phenomenal properties with that target experience. In which case, if those resemblances are non-trivial then someone might come to possess useful silver WIL-knowledge of the target experience based on their having had the simulation experience.

This is not to say, of course, that any given attempt by someone to gain WIL-knowledge of other people's experiences using a VR simulation – or testimony, literature, and so on – will result in that person gaining partial WIL-knowledge. For as Bloom (2017), Ngo (2017a), and Ramirez (2021) and others point out, such attempts can sometimes lead us to false beliefs about what the relevant target experience is like, in which case those beliefs will not constitute knowledge at all. The point is simply that we cannot infer from the assumed impossibility of using VR to gain experience entailing forms of WIL-knowledge that it is also impossible to use VR to gain partial and non-experience entailing forms of WIL-knowledge. And the same point applies to any method of forming beliefs about what it is like to have an experience that does not involve having the target experience oneself.

Relatedly, it would be a mistake to infer from the fact that there can be significant variations in how the same event or action of Φ-ing can make different people feel, due to differences in who they are, that there cannot be significant patterns and similarities in how different people feel when they Φ. There is such a thing, after all, as 'shared experiences' and it would be an extremely sceptical position to maintain that people can only be said to have shared experiences, and shared experiential knowledge, when they have the exact same experiences due to their having the exact same intersectional identities and psychological dispositions and so on, as that would effectively mean that people almost never have shared experiences and shared experiential knowledge. Consider two friends who are both members of a student LGBTQIA+ group. They may differ in their gender identities and sexual orientations, and they might have different class, cultural, and race experiences, and psychological dispositions, and so on. In which case, following Ramirez's intersectional theory of experience, any of those differences could cause them to experience the same events in significantly different ways. But, nonetheless, they might still find value and solidarity in certain significant similarities in their distinct experiences of, say, navigating heteronormative cultures in the university, or coming out to their families, even whilst acknowledging and learning from each other that there are also important differences in their respective experiences. And in this qualified sense these two people could be said to have 'shared experiences' and shared WIL-knowledge with respect to the overlaps in their distinct but partially similar experiences.[12]

The extent to which we can gain different forms of partial WIL-knowledge through activities that do not involve having the relevant target experience – like consulting literature, testimony, simulations, or theories – is an interesting and difficult question, and one that I think we should approach on a careful case-by-case basis. Authors like Bloom, Ngo, and Ramirez show us that there are significant epistemic pitfalls that we can fall into in trying to gain WIL-knowledge through using simulations, and other authors, like Berninger (2023), have identified related dangers with respect to testimony. The insights of these authors remind us that we should approach any attempt to learn about experiences we have not had with a great deal of epistemic humility and with due deference to the epistemic authority of those who have had experiences of that type. But we should not let the intuitive plausibility of the experience condition trick us into thinking that all such attempts are doomed to be epistemically fruitless just because they can't provide us with the actual experiences they aim to illuminate.

6.4 Combination Concerns

Another related worry one might have with the idea of partial WIL-knowledge is that even if one has had an experience which shares certain experiential parts with the given target experience, one still can't know that the total experiential parts of the target experience won't combine in unexpected ways. Furthermore, such worries might seem compounded by the fact that we still have such a poor theoretical understanding of how experiential parts combine into whole experiences, and the principles governing these mereological relations (see, e.g., Lee 2014; Koksvik 2014).[13]

There are many interesting issues one could explore concerning the relation between partial WIL-knowledge and the mereological properties of our experiences. But given the scope of this discussion, I will limit myself here to explaining why I think that such explorations are unlikely to support any deep scepticism about the, in principle, possibility of achieving forms of partial WIL-knowledge.

Firstly, we shouldn't infer from the mere fact that we have a poor theoretical understanding of the principles governing how experiential parts compose larger experiences, that partial WIL-knowledge is impossible. For the general

---

[12] See Allen (2022: 1127) for related discussion.

[13] Thanks to a reviewer and to Walter Pedriali who both pressed me to address these concerns.

idea that a belief forming process can only lead us to knowledge if we also have further explicit knowledge of how it works, and the principles it relies upon, is an implausibly demanding condition that risks leading us into deep forms of scepticism. And, more specifically, such a stance about partial WIL-knowledge would force us to reject apparently clear cases of such knowledge. So, for example, I have never had the experience of eating a kiwifruit whilst walking down Sydney Road. Nonetheless, I think I still have good, albeit partial, knowledge of what it is like to have that experience, at least in normal circumstances. For I have eaten kiwifruit in many other settings, and I have walked down Sydney Road many times. So, given these experiences, I can form quite accurate imaginings and beliefs concerning what it is like to have this target experience which I have not had.

In this example I make a 'normal circumstances' qualification. But what about less normal circumstances? As Koksvik (2014: 115) points out, even the experiences of a routine walk can be dramatically altered when they are had in combination with an intense mood:

> Even going for a familiar walk can be a very different experience in a buoyant mood. It is as if the good feeling bleeds into every other experience: even mundane things *look* sparkly and full of promise at those times, utterly different from their grey and hopeless appearance in negative moods.

However, as Koksvik also notes, most of us have experienced how intense moods can alter familiar experiences. So, I think I can still have reasonable, albeit partial, knowledge of what it is like to eat a kiwifruit whilst walking down Sydney Road in a mood of high elation, based on my experiences of elated moods in other situations. And we shouldn't overestimate the degree to which our moods alter other experiences. There will usually still be significant similarities between, for example, the visual phenomenology of the walk in a normal mood and the same walk in a mood of intense elation. After all, while an elated mood might transform a walk from being dull to being enchanting, it typically won't result in one's getting lost.

On the other hand, having never taken psychedelic drugs, I may not be in a position to have any even partial knowledge of what it is like to eat a kiwifruit when walking down Sydney Road as part of a larger psychedelic experience. Or if I can gain *some* such knowledge, it will be thin and uninformative with respect to what makes psychedelic experiences so distinctive. For I am not familiar with psychedelic experiences and how they combine with, and dramatically alter, otherwise familiar experiences.

Perhaps we should view our attempts at understanding the experiences of other people in different social locations as being a similar kind of case? The idea being that even if there are some relevant similarities between the experiences of two people in different social locations, the total parts of their respective experiences will combine in very different ways and to such an extent that neither person can achieve any even partial WIL-knowledge of the other's experiences (or at least no non-trivial forms of such knowledge). There may be specific cases where this is the right conclusion to reach. But it would be very implausible to generalise this idea to all cases where people are in different social locations. For such a position would, again, commit one to the implausible claim that in the LGBTQIA+ student case that it is impossible for either student to achieve any even partial WIL-knowledge with respect to the experiences of their friend.

Furthermore, while testimony may do a poor job of conveying the phenomenal character of experiences that are radically different from any of our previous experiences, it can at least inform us that there are these significant differences. And, more generally, testimony can alert us to all kinds of potential errors we might make in our assessments of a target experience based on our familiarity with some, but not all, of its experiential parts; including mistaken judgements about how those experiential parts combine with other experiential parts of the target experience. And the fact that there are such means for detecting these errors is another reason for cautious optimism about our abilities to sometimes achieve forms of partial WIL-knowledge. For this suggests that the serious errors we can make in trying to achieve partial WIL-knowledge are best viewed not as insurmountable barriers, but challenges, which we can manage and sometimes overcome.

7 Conclusions

There is a prima facie tension between the answer and experience conditions, as the answer condition pushes us to think of WIL-knowledge as a form of propositional knowledge, whereas the experience condition might seem to push towards thinking that WIL-knowledge is some kind of non-propositional knowledge, like ability or acquaintance knowledge. However, in this Element I argued that, ultimately, this tension can be resolved by thinking of interrogative WIL-knowledge as a form of downstream knowledge which involves the possession of abilities to imagine and recognise experiences. I also showed how WIL-knowledge on this view can come in different degrees, and how that fact can illuminate the initially puzzling relationship between WIL-knowledge and testimony. And, finally, I briefly explored some of the possibilities and pitfalls involved in trying to acquire partial WIL-knowledge of experiences one has not had oneself.

References

Allen, P. (2022). Experience, knowledge, and political representation. *Politics & Gender*, 18 (4): 1112–1140.

Alter, T. (2001). Know-how, ability, and the ability hypothesis. *Theoria*, 67 (3): 229–239.

Ball, D. (2009). There are no phenomenal concepts. *Mind*, 118 (472): 935–962.

Berninger, A. (2023). Experience and understanding in response to holocaust testimony. In T. Petraschka and C. Werner, eds., *Empathy's Role in Understanding Persons, Literature, and Art*, New York: Routledge, pp. 84–102.

Bloom, P. (2017). It's ridiculous to use virtual reality to empathize with refugees. *The Atlantic*. www.theatlantic.com/technology/archive/2017/02/virtual-reality-wont-make-you-more-empathetic/515511/.

Carter, J. A. and J. Navarro. (2017). The defeasibility of knowledge-how. *Philosophy and Phenomenological Research*, 95: 662–85.

Cath, Y. (2011). Knowing how without knowing that. In J. Bengson and M. Moffett, eds., *Knowing How: Essays on Knowledge, Mind, and Action*, Oxford: Oxford University Press, pp. 113–135.

Cath, Y. (2019). Knowing what it is like and testimony. *Australasian Journal of Philosophy*, 97 (1): 105–120.

Cath, Y. (2020). Know how and skill: The puzzles of priority and equivalence. In E. Fridland & C. Pavese, eds., *Routledge Handbook of the Philosophy of Skill and Expertise*, New York: Routledge, pp. 157–167.

Cath, Y. (2022). Transformative experiences and the equivocation objection. *Inquiry*, 1–22. https://doi.org/10.1080/0020174X.2022.2107063.

Cath, Y. (2023). Expanding the client's perspective. *Philosophical Quarterly*, 73 (3): 701–721.

Cawston, A. and Wildman, N. (2023). Are you (relevantly) experienced? A moral argument for video games. In L. D'Olimpio, P. Paris, and A. P. Thompson, eds., *Educating Character through the Arts*, London: Routledge, pp. 109–124.

Chappell, S. G. (2017). *Knowing What to Do: Imagination, Virtue, and Platonism in Ethics*, Oxford: Oxford University Press.

Coleman, S. (2009). Why the ability hypothesis is best forgotten. *Journal of Consciousness Studies*, 16 (2–3): 74–97.

Conee, E. (1994). Phenomenal knowledge. *Australasian Journal of Philosophy*, 72 (2): 136–150.

Craig, E. (1990). *Knowledge and the State of Nature*, Oxford: Oxford University Press.

Currie, G. (2020). *Imagining and Knowing: The Shape of Fiction*, Oxford: Oxford University Press.

D'Ambrosio, J. and Stoljar, D. (2021). Vendler's puzzle about imagination. *Synthese*, 199 (5–6): 2923–2944.

Duncan, M. (2021). Acquaintance. *Philosophy Compass*, 16 (3): 1–19.

Farkas, K. (2019). Objectual knowledge. In T. Raleigh and J. Knowles, eds., *Acquaintance: New Essays*, Oxford: Oxford University Press. pp. 260–276.

Fürst, M. (2023). Closing the conceptual gap in epistemic injustice. *The Philosophical Quarterly*, 74 (1): 229–250.

Ginet, C. (1975). *Knowledge, Perception, and Memory*, Dordrecht: D. Reidel.

Glick, E. (2015). Practical Modes of Presentation. *Noûs*, 49 (3): 538–559.

Grzankowski, A. and Tye, M. (2019). What acquaintance teaches. In T. Raleigh and J. Knowles, eds., *Acquaintance: New Essays*, Oxford: Oxford University Press, pp. 75–94.

Hawley, K. (2011). Knowing how and epistemic injustice. In J. Bengson and M. Moffett, eds., *Knowing How: Essays on Knowledge, Mind, and Action*, Oxford: Oxford University Press, pp. 283–299.

Hookway, C. (2006). Epistemology and inquiry: The primacy of practice. In S. Hetherington, ed., *Epistemology Futures*, Oxford: Oxford University Press.

Jackson, F. (1982). Epiphenomenal Qualia. *Philosophical Quarterly*, 32: 127–136.

Kind, A. (2020). What imagination teaches. In J. Schwenkler and E. Lambert, eds., *Becoming Someone New: Essays on Transformative Experience, Choice, and Change*, Oxford: Oxford University Press, pp. 133–146.

Kind, A. (2021). Bridging the divide: Imagining across experiential perspectives. In C. Badura and A, Kind, eds., *Epistemic Uses of Imagination*, New York: Routledge, pp. 237–259.

Koksvik, O. (2014). Three models of phenomenal unity. *Journal of Consciousness Studies*, 21 (7–8): 105–131.

Lee, A. Y. (2023). Knowing what it's like. *Philosophical Perspectives*, 37 (1): 187–209.

Lee, G. (2014). Experiences and their parts. In B. Hill, ed., *Sensory Integration and the Unity of Consciousness*, Boston: MIT Press, pp. 287–381.

Lewis, D. (1988). What experience teaches. Reprinted in P. Ludlow, Y. Nagasawa, and D. Stoljar, eds. (2004). *There's Something about Mary: Essays on Phenomenal Consciousness and Frank Jackson's Knowledge Argument*, Boston: MIT Press, pp. 77–103.

Lycan, W. G. (1996). *Consciousness and Experience*, Cambridge, MA: MIT Press.

Nemirow, L. (1990). Physicalism and the cognitive role of acquaintance. In W. Lycan, ed., *Mind and Cognition*, Cambridge: Basil Blackwell, pp. 490–499.

Nemirow, L. (2006). So *this* is what it's like: A defense of the ability hypothesis. In T.A. Alter and S. Walter, eds., *Phenomenal Concepts and Phenomenal Knowledge: New Essays on Consciousness and Physicalism*, Oxford: Oxford University Press, pp. 32–51.

Ngo, H. (2017a). Simulating the lived experience of racism and islamophobia: On 'embodied empathy' and political tourism. *Australian Feminist Law Journal*, 43 (1): 107–123.

Ngo, H. (2017b). *The Habits of Racism: A Phenomenology of Racism and Racialized Embodiment*, Maryland: Lexington Books.

Paul, L. A. (2014). *Transformative Experience*, Oxford: Oxford University Press.

Paul, L. A. (2015a). What you can't expect when you're expecting. *Res Philosophica*, 92 (2): 1–23.

Paul, L. A. (2015b). Transformative choice: Discussion and replies. *Res Philosophica*, 92 (2): 473–545.

Pavese, C. (2015). Practical senses. *Philosophers' Imprint*, 15 (29): 1–25.

Pavese, C. (2017). Know-how and gradability. *Philosophical Review*, 126 (3): 345–383.

Poston, T. (2009). Know how to be gettiered? *Philosophy and Phenomenological Research*, 79 (3): 743–747.

Poston, T. (2016). Know how to transmit knowledge? *Noûs*, 50 (4): 865–878.

Ramirez, E. (2018, October). It's dangerous to think virtual reality is an empathy machine. *Aeon*. https://aeon.co/ideas/its-dangerous-to-think-virtual-reality-is-an-empathy-machine.

Ramirez, E. J. (2021). *The Ethics of Virtual and Augmented Reality: Building Worlds*, New York: Routledge.

Russell, B. (1911). Knowledge by acquaintance and knowledge by description. *Proceedings of the Aristotelian Society*, 11: 108–128.

Ryle, G. (1949). *The Concept of Mind*, Chicago: University of Chicago Press.

Sainsbury, R. M. and Tye, M. (2012). *Seven Puzzles of Thought and How to Solve Them: An Originalist Theory of Concepts*, New York: Oxford University Press.

Schwitzgebel, E. (2013). A dispositional approach to the attitudes. In N. Nottelmann, ed., *New Essays on Belief*, New York: Palgrave Macmillan. pp. 75–99.

Sherman, N. (2010). *The Untold War: Inside the Hearts and Minds and Souls of Our Soldiers*, New York: W.W. Norton.

Stanley, J. (2011). *Know How*, New York: Oxford University Press.

Stanley, J. and Williamson, T. (2001). Knowing how. *Journal of Philosophy*, 98: 411–444.

Stoljar, D. (2015). Lewis on materialism and experience. In B. Loewer and J. Schaffer, eds., *A Companion to David Lewis*, Chichester: John Wiley & Sons, pp. 519–532.

Stoljar, D. (2016). The semantics of 'what it's like' and the nature of consciousness. *Mind*, 125 (500): 1161–1198.

Sundström, P. (2011). Phenomenal concepts. *Philosophy Compass*, 6 (4): 267–281.

Tye, M. (2000). Knowing what it is like: The ability hypothesis and the knowledge argument. In G. Preyer, eds., *Reality and Humean Supervenience: Essays on the Philosophy of David Lewis*, Lanham: Rowman & Littlefield, pp. 223–238.

Tye, M. (2011). Knowing what it is like. In J. Bengson and M. Moffett, eds., *Knowing How: Essays on Knowledge, Mind, and Action*, Oxford: Oxford University Press, pp. 300–313.

Waights Hickman, N. (2019). Knowing in the 'executive way': Knowing how, rules, methods, principles and criteria. *Philosophy and Phenomenological Research*, 99 (2): 311–335.

Werner, C. (2023). 'Tell me, how does it feel?': Learning what it is like through literature. In T. Petraschka and C. Werner, eds., *Empathy's Role in Understanding Persons, Literature, and Art*, New York: Routledge, pp. 174–196.

Zagzebski, L. (2008). Omnisubjectivity. In J. Kvanvig, ed., *Oxford Studies in Philosophy of Religion*, Oxford: Oxford University Press, pp. 231–248.

Zhou, N. (2017, June). CEO Sleepout criticised as 'dystopian' for homeless simulation with VR headsets. *The Guardian: Australia Edition*. www.the guardian.com/australia-news/2017/jun/23/ceo-sleepout-criticised-as-dys topian-for-homeless-simulation-with-vr-headsets.

Acknowledgements

I am grateful to two anonymous reviewers for their insightful suggestions which improved this Element. My thanks also to Stephen Hetherington for his encouragement, and to audiences at the ANU for helpful feedback on an early draft of Sections 1–4, especially Andrew Y. Lee and Daniel Stoljar.

Cambridge Elements ≣

Epistemology

Stephen Hetherington
University of New South Wales, Sydney

Stephen Hetherington is Professor Emeritus of Philosophy at the University of New South Wales, Sydney. He is the author of numerous books, including *Knowledge and the Gettier Problem* (Cambridge University Press, 2016), and *What Is Epistemology?* (Polity, 2019), and is the editor several others, including *Knowledge in Contemporary Epistemology* (with Markos Valaris: Bloomsbury, 2019), and *What the Ancients Offer to Contemporary Epistemology* (with Nicholas D. Smith: Routledge, 2020). He was the Editor-in-Chief of the Australasian Journal of Philosophy from 2013 until 2022.

About the Series

This Elements series seeks to cover all aspects of a rapidly evolving field, including emerging and evolving topics such as: fallibilism; knowinghow; self-knowledge; knowledge of morality; knowledge and injustice; formal epistemology; knowledge and religion; scientific knowledge; collective epistemology; applied epistemology; virtue epistemology; wisdom. The series demonstrates the liveliness and diversity of the field, while also pointing to new areas of investigation.

Cambridge Elements $\equiv$

Epistemology

Printed in the United States
by Baker & Taylor Publisher Services